John Dobbert's
FIRST AID for Marriage

VISION HOUSE PUBLISHERS
Santa Ana, California 92705

Except where otherwise noted, all Scripture quotations are taken from The Living Bible, Copyright 1971 by Tyndale House Publishers, Wheaton, Illinois. Used by permission.

Verses marked NASB are taken from The New American Standard Bible, Copyright © The Lockman Foundation 1960, 1962, 1963, 1968, 1971. Used by permission.

First Aid for Marriage

Copyright © 1978 by Vision House Publishers, Santa Ana, California 92705.

Library of Congress Catalog Card Number 78-56106
ISBN 0-88449-036-X

All rights reserved. No portion of this book may be reproduced in any form without the written permission of the Publishers, except for brief excerpts in reviews.

Printed in the United States of America.

To Dottie, my beloved wife,
and
Wayne and Carol Bennett,
who have shared their lives
to enrich ours

I gratefully acknowledge the assistance and input received from my dear friend, Richard Charlebois.

Thanks also to my marriage encounter community for some ideas contained herein.

CONTENTS

	Introduction	7
1.	First Aid for Marriage	9
2.	"I'll Never Need First Aid"	13
3.	Who is Best Equipped?	19
4.	The Prevention Program	23
5.	Necessary Attributes	27
6.	How to Handle Adversity	33
7.	Choking (Stifling Your Mate)	47
8.	Frostbite (Disinterest in Your Mate)	57
9.	Burns (Downgrading Your Mate)	69
10.	Eye Injury (Inability to View Your Relationship Clearly)	85
11.	Shock (Withdrawal or Failure to Respond	95
12.	Poisoning (Reckless Words or Acts)	101
13.	Drug Abuse (Foreign Substances)	107
14.	Heart Attack (Blockages to Keep from Exposing the Real You)	113

15.	Drowning (Wallowing in Self-Pity)	121
16.	Heat Exhaustion (When You've Got No More to Give)	127
17.	Check Your First-Aid Kit	133
18.	Timely Techniques	137
19.	If First Aid Fails	169
20.	First-Aid Priorities	173
21.	Prescription of the Great Physician	177

INTRODUCTION

The divine institution of marriage has fallen on hard times. Maintaining a marriage has become for many couples an impossible task. Estimates indicate that more than one million couples will file for divorce this year, and some ministers actually report more divorces than marriages within their fellowship!

During the last decade, a liberal, pleasure-seeking philosophy has contributed to the deterioration of marriage by encouraging open marriage, living together, experimental marriage, extramarital relationships, multiple marriages, and a "do-your-own-thing" philosophy which has in general endorsed every activity leading to immediate gratification without accompanying commitment. This philosophy, if adopted, views everything and every person as expendable.

Divorce and discontent in marriage are no respecters of persons. Black, white, yellow, red; rich, poor, professionally successful or unsuccessful; atheist, Baptist, Mormon, Presbyterian, Catholic; newly married or seasoned couples—all are vitally affected by the inability to maintain any marriage relationship at all, much less one characterized by richness and fullness.

And just as sad as the divorce statistics are those additional millions of people who reside as man and wife under the same roof but at gut level have been mentally and emotionally separated for years.

Don't concede to the daily pressures and temptations to terminate your relationship. This book offers a thorough but simple explanation of techniques which you and your mate can master and apply, to allow your relationship to far exceed your every expectation.

CHAPTER 1
FIRST AID FOR MARRIAGE

> When someone is injured or suddenly becomes ill, there is a critical period—before you can get medical help—that is of the utmost importance to the victim. What you do, or what you *don't* do, in that interval can mean the difference between life and death. For serious conditions it is vitally important to get the patient to a doctor. You will always find one at the emergency room of the nearest hospital. If you cannot take the patient there, call an ambulance at once. First aid is the help that you can provide until professional help takes over. You owe it to yourself, your family and your neighbors to know and to understand the simple procedures which can be applied, quickly and intelligently, in an emergency.*

This definition of first aid may at first glance seem irrelevant to a discussion about marriage relationships, but if that is your assessment, I challenge you to reread the definition five times, searching each word open-mindedly in an effort to discover some correlation between first aid and the marriage relationship.

---

*Reprinted with permission from the "Reader's Digest Handbook of First Aid." © 1975 The Reader's Digest Association, Inc.

Is your marriage relationship already injured? Was that injury incurred abruptly through one vicious attack while you were under considerable stress? Or was it a premeditated and carefully planned attack designed to terminate the relationship? Or was the injury sustained slowly, over a long period of time, through a series of subtly inconsiderate acts?

Is your relationship ill? Physical illness may range from a short-lived stomach upset to a serious lingering illness, and marriage-relationship illness may vary in severity as well.

That illness may have been caused by an external agent (someone outside the relationship), but more likely it was caused by an internal agent (one or both of the marriage partners themselves).

If you are ill or the victim of a physical accident, you must carefully examine the resulting symptoms to determine the course of action to be taken. The severity of the illness or injury will determine how the patient or patients must be treated. There is a critical period that is most important to the victim of a physical injury or illness. Acting promptly to treat the victim may allow the injury to heal, thus eliminating the necessity for prolonged professional help.

Acting promptly when a couple recognizes the symptoms in a status quo or deteriorating marriage relationship can also halt further deterioration and can provide a chance to remedy the situation without professional counseling assistance.

When physical injury is extremely serious, the first-aider's sole responsibility is to provide assistance until the doctor takes over. He should never exceed the limit of his training, since his actions may result in increased injury and even permanent disability.

The marriage relationship is similar. When the couple recognizes that their relationship is about to be severed despite the fact that they have attempted to use all techniques at their disposal, certainly professional counseling should be sought.

What the first-aider does or doesn't do could make the difference between life or death for the victim of a physical injury, and the victims of a faltering marriage relationship are offered a similar prognosis. They must recognize the deteriorating condition of their marriage and decide on an immediate course of action, the success of which could mean life or death to their relationship.

The first-aid kit, with concise and easy-to-understand instructions for proper application, is mandatory for a person assisting the victim of a physical illness or injury. Your first-aid kit for marriage is found in the subsequent chapters of this book. I hope that you will find the marriage-relationship danger symptoms easy to detect, the treatments clearly explained, and the applications effective.

You owe it to your family, your neighbors, your friends, and yourself to understand and be able to apply the strategies discussed in this book.

This book will draw many comparisons between physical problems and marital problems, which will illuminate your pathway to marriage fullness. I have great hopes for your relationship. I believe that by using the techniques contained in this book, you and your marriage relationship can far exceed the expectations which most first-aiders have for the people they help.

I have seen many dying relationships revived, many faltering relationships recovered, and many good relationships become great. I am convinced that all marriage partners who are willing to learn and to exert maximum effort can enjoy a richly blossoming marriage. Don't sell short the possibilities of your own marriage until you have finished this book!

CHAPTER 2

"I'LL NEVER NEED FIRST AID"

Almost everyone goes through life requiring physical first aid several times along the way. It is simply naive to think we can escape unscathed from physical injuries for an entire lifetime.

It is equally naive to think that our marriage is ideal, and cannot be improved. An ideal marriage may exist, but I've certainly never seen one. Actually, as we view a marriage from the outside it may appear to be anything from excellent to disastrous, but only the participants can truly judge the quality of their marriage.

Idealness sometimes becomes a self-adjustable standard; a mediocre marriage can be considered ideal if the partners are satisfied with the level of fulfillment they receive from it. On the other hand, a good marriage can be considered far from ideal if the partners desire a level of fullness beyond that which they're currently receiving. Each couple possess standards of expectation for their own relationship.

As a principal of a large secondary school, I see an increasing number of students adjusting their scholastic standards downward, so that they gain pseudosatisfaction with "C" grades when their past performance shows that earning an "A" would be a distinct possibility.

In counseling these students we can observe a profile characterized by:

1. lack of fulfillment.
2. dissatisfaction with their own performance.
3. striving for recognition and acceptance in some alternate manner (often socially unacceptable).
4. a poor self-concept.

The marriage relationship can be beset by the same problems as the partners bury their heads in the sand, claiming "ideal relationship—no need for first aid" while dropping their standard in an attempt to believe their statement and justify their false claim.

If you can't improve the relationship, why not lower the standard of expectation by which the relationship is judged?

Just as the potential "A" student earning "C" was dissatisfied and lacked fulfillment, the potential "A" marriage relationship earning "C" will be marked by an absence of satisfaction and fulfillment in the partners involved.

Remember, the world's standard for marriage is very low, so when you compare your marriage with others around you, yours may look pretty good even though it is vastly inferior to what it could be.

Married couples have the same capacity for living a lie in front of people as individuals do. During a loud argument with your mate, have you ever been interrupted by a visitor's knock, only to respond in a sweet voice and pleasant demeanor, "Why, hello there, how are you?"

The visitor is unaware of the tumultuous scene he interrupted or the pseudotranquility he brought into the residence, unless he has been gifted with keen perception or picks up hints during the ensuing conversation.

Spectators to a marriage are likened to a visitor, for truly they may be viewing two actors in dress rehearsal who, although presenting the public image of an excellent and communicative marriage, are actually tearing at each other viciously in the privacy of their own home.

Even more dangerous and difficult to detect is the insidious intrusion of subtle destructive behavior patterns wedging themselves almost undetected between the marriage partners.

You may believe your marriage is healthy until you evaluate your relationship in light of the information in this book.

Have you ever been flabbergasted when a couple you thought had an excellent marriage filed for divorce? Have you ever viewed a volatile relationship over a period of time, expecting an announcement of an impending divorce which never came?

Maybe we're not as perceptive as we believe we are. In addition, our limited perception is colored by our emotions. We may be seeing what we want and expect to see rather than the signals which are actually being given, thus greatly limiting the accuracy of our perception.

Every marriage relationship has many characteristics, emotions, and problems known only to the partners involved, or perhaps only to one of the partners and to his or her Creator.

But this book is not written to help you evaluate *other people's* relationships; it is written to help you improve your *own* marriage.

And I believe without equivocation that every relationship *can* be improved. Whether your marriage is in imminent danger, or your marriage is the greatest example of perfection on record, or your relationship lies somewhere between these two extremes, *the relationship can be improved.*

How much?

Your relationship can be improved as much as you desire, if you are willing to candidly evaluate your relationship, to recognize the symptoms of a stale or dissipating relationship, and to implement the strategies contained in this book. If you take these steps, your marriage can explode into fullness.

If you believe that your marriage can't be improved, you either—

1. know that your relationship is completely devoid of love.
2. are naive to the point of absurdity.
3. won't admit that your relationship could be improved.
4. are too lazy to expend the energy required.
5. believe that your partner (and children, if any) don't merit your attempts at improvement.
6. seriously doubt your worth as an individual.
7. have never been made aware of the techniques explained in this book.

Although an outside accrediting team might rate your marriage as "fairly good to average," you may know that such is not the case.

Your marriage may be slipping into a noncommunicating coexistence, a trend which both of you may dread but neither know how to reverse.

Your conversation or thoughts may be focused on the probing question, "When the kids are gone, do we really want to spend the remaining years of our life together?"

This question may be unanswerable right now, but if

both of you are willing to make a commitment to renewal, you have taken the first giant step.

In a matter of months, your marriage could explode into fullness—fullness marked not just by words but by action, concern, consideration, joy, sharing, empathy, emotional and sexual fulfillment, spiritual oneness, and everything good.

I would like to share with you those strategies that will result in just such an explosion of marital fullness.

CHAPTER 3
WHO IS BEST EQUIPPED?

A psychologist named Robert Carkhuff surveyed research studying the effectiveness of "lay helpers." He concluded that when lay counselors, with or without training, were compared with professionals, it was discovered that "the patients of lay counselors do as well as or better than the patients of professional counselors."*

Carkhuff also concluded that when a professional counselor first began receiving his training he did a better job in helping people than the laymen, but as training continued the professional counselor became less effective and frequently ended up doing a worse job than the untrained lay counselor.

As an educator I often observe the success which peer counselors are experiencing in our secondary public schools. Many students are being positively affected even though professional counselors have failed to reach them.

People close to the counseling field have theorized that Carkhuff's findings were true because—

---

*From page 117 of R. R. Carkhuff's "Differential Functioning of Lay and Professional Helpers," in *Journal of Counseling Psychology*, vol. 15, 1968.

1. the lay helper or peer counselor is closer to the helpee and therefore better able to understand and empathize with his or her problem.
2. the lay helper often knows the helpee personally.
3. the lay helper is readily available.
4. the lay helper communicates on the same level as the person needing help.
5. the lay helper can be approached informally without the helpee being threatened with office visits, degrees, status, or stigma.
6. the lay helper is more practical and less concerned with theory, procedures, or trying new techniques.

The best helpers are often the people known, respected, and loved by the person needing help.

Marcia Lasswell and Norman Lobsenz in their book *No-Fault Marriage* state, "Certainly no struggle is more common than marriage, and no comrade closer than a wife or husband. Thus, for a couple to work together on their relationship, to be their own therapists, seems both logical and fitting. It is also likely to be highly effective once the necessary skills are mastered."*

They continue by saying, "We believe that, by learning the fundamental techniques that counselors use and then learning how to apply them in your own marriage, you can, to a considerable extent, do for yourself what a counselor would help you to do."*

Numerous seminars are conducted locally and nationally to teach couples techniques allowing them to play the vital role of counselor in order to improve their own marriage relationship.

---

*Excerpts from *No-Fault Marriage*, by Marcia Lasswell and Norman M. Lobsenz. Copyright © 1976 by Marcia Lasswell and Norman M. Lobsenz. For use by permission of Doubleday & Company, Inc.

I contend that you and your mate are in the best position of anyone on this earth to apply first aid to your marriage relationship and to make it an exciting, fulfilling experience.

The techniques you need to master in order to make this self-counseling highly effective are explained in detail in the chapters which follow.

CHAPTER 4

THE PREVENTION PROGRAM

When it comes to first aid, we often hear the motto, "Prevention is the best cure," and that is certainly true. We are encouraged to—

1. keep poison in a locked cabinet out of children's reach.
2. keep sharp objects out of children's reach.
3. not leave objects on staircases.
4. have the entire family wear seat belts in the vehicle.
5. make certain swimming pool areas are locked.
6. never swim alone.
7. install smoke alarms in our home.

Countless other examples could be cited which encourage us to take preventive measures in order to avoid physical injuries.

These and other examples of preventive steps will not totally eliminate the need for first aid, but they will certainly reduce the number of times first aid must be rendered.

When we don't heed the request to examine our homes, cars, and offices in order to correct existing situations which are potentially dangerous, we are saying by our inaction that we would rather take our chances on more serious injury than exert the necessary effort to correct the situation.

When injury then befalls us or a member of our family due to our neglect, remorse hangs heavy on our minds because we know that the injury could easily have been avoided.

Pain has now entered the picture, and treatment is required to prevent further complications, increased pain, or even death.

The marriage relationship affords a chance to invoke a prevention program as well.

Although you are not bombarded with TV spots, messages by the Red Cross, or safety campaigns and posters (as in the area of physical accident avoidance), you should be aware that neglecting preventive measures in your marriage relationship can result in serious problems.

These problems, although not usually inflicting *physical* pain, can inflict severe mental and emotional pain with all their associated physical problems. If the problems are allowed to continue unchecked, the relationship can ultimately die.

Wouldn't it be far wiser to take the preventive steps *now*, while your marriage relationship is still fair to good, than try to revive a dead relationship at a later date?

Most of the techniques necessary to prevent injury or illness from occurring in your marriage are detailed in Chapter 18, but some basic measures that you can work on right now are listed below.

1. Establish priorities for your relationship. Give it first place in time and effort.
2. Schedule a daily time together to sit down and communicate.

3. Nurture hobbies together.
4. Plan together.
5. Pray together. Praying about mutual concerns brings two people closer.
6. Always expect the best of each other. Have confidence in each other.
7. Extol the virtues of your mate.
8. Realistically appraise the weaknesses you see in your mate.
9. Cater to each other's needs.
10. Commit your relationship in love to Christ.

CHAPTER 5
NECESSARY ATTRIBUTES

Love

It was obvious that the accident victim was suffocating in his own vomit, whereupon two of the bystanders turned away in revulsion. The other bystander, however, took his handkerchief and cleared the victim's mouth as best he could, after which he began oral resuscitation.

As I read the account of this true incident, I was impressed that a perfect stranger was so filled with concern for his fellowman that he thought nothing of the stench and unsanitary conditions of the suffering victim, but instead plunged ahead and breathed life into an unlovely creature.

You may say, "Gross." I say, "Beautiful." The willingness to assist a victim of an accident or sudden illness is an expression of love. In order to extend the hand of love, we must possess love within our being.

If genuine love for mankind had not been present, the third stranger would also have taken the easy way out, just as the other two observers did.

A marriage relationship is much the same. The partners involved may be aware of problems in their relationship, but unless underlying love exists, it is unlikely that either spouse will make the commitment and effort required to improve the situation. Walking away from an injured relationship leaves it to struggle and possibly die.

Empathy, although interrelated with love, isn't exactly the same as love. Empathy says, "I care," and care is a real comfort to a hurting person. Empathy also says, "I'm reaching out and trying my best to give you what you need."

The general rule seems to be that the quality of the treatment, whether in first aid or marriage, is proportional to the amount of love and empathy which the giver possesses.

Love can be conveyed to an absolute stranger by your willingness to render assistance, and love should also be evident to your spouse through your dedicated attempts to improve the marriage relationship.

Training

If you were injured and profusely bleeding, would you rather be helped by a well-schooled first-aider or by a person devoid of all first-aid training?

The answer is obvious: we tend to have much more confidence in a person whose skills are evident as he encounters the situation, for the chances of successful treatment are greatly enhanced when assistance is rendered by a well-trained person.

Shortly after our plane was in the air, headed for Chicago, an elderly lady ten rows in front of us slumped toward her window. A moment of panic ensued as the stewardess and flight attendant rushed to her seat. The determination was made that she was in imminent danger of death. In a few seconds, the flight attendant grabbed the microphone and issued the following statement: "If there is a doctor on the plane, please report to row 40." Three hundred people were on the plane, and certainly many of them were caring individuals, yet only the person with training could help in this life-or-death situation. A doctor arrived at row 40 and administered a drug in an attempt to maintain life, but it was too late.

If a doctor had not been on the plane, many people would have wondered if she could have been saved if only a doctor had been on board. We place a premium on training.

These truths find application in our marriage relationship as well. As partners we can be more successful in assisting each other (and therefore our relationship) when we possess skills obtained through training.

This training need not be formal; some of us are trained by reading, others by participating in in-service weekends, others at couples' conferences, and still others through a variety of activities or courses.

"Demands on our time" is frequently used as an excuse for not being trained, yet a half-hour a day in our own home will assist us greatly in achieving a level of training sufficient to greatly affect the quality of our marriage. Once trained, however, we must realize that skills obtained can become outdated or can even be lost due to non-use.

Updating these skills through seminars, reading, and continued experimentation and use helps us to keep our skills sharp and to maintain our abilities.

Willingness and Commitment to Use Training

A skillfully trained first-aider who fails to use his skill is as worthless as a surgeon who faints at the sight of blood.

Knowledge without the commitment to apply that knowledge toward constructive ends is a sham.

You may have graduated at the top of your Red Cross class, but without commitment to use that training you might as well have been a habitual truant.

No better prognosis exists for marriage partners who have read all the books and taken all the courses but have no commitment toward those valuable techniques which will improve their relationship. In his book entitled *The Greatest Salesman in the World,* Og Mandino states, "My dreams are worthless, my plans are dust, my goals are impossible. All are of no value unless they are followed by action. I will act now."

Confidence, Calmness, and Clear-headedness

If you seriously doubt your ability to render assistance to people, your effectiveness will be lessened.

Lack of confidence is often responsible for choosing the wrong course of action.

In first-aid emergencies, treating a related injury, such as splinting a fractured arm, while overlooking the more serious immediate danger involving difficulty in breathing can mean sudden death for the victim. Your ability to be calm and rational under pressure will allow you to make the correct decision and will also allow you to reassure the victim that you know what you are doing. A reassured and confident victim is much easier to treat than one who doubts your ability to treat him.

Choosing the wrong course of action in a marital emergency (for example, extended silence rather than increased communication after an argument) can lead to increased marital problems, and even marital death.

Attentiveness

It is extremely important that a first-aider listen carefully to the injured but conscious victim, since his description of how the accident occurred and the location of the injury often assists in determining the proper treatment. Attentiveness in the marriage relationship is just as vitally important. The skill of listening to one's mate and hearing what he or she really says is of utmost importance in treating the problem correctly.

Occasionally one doubts his ability to help, since he has not been professionally trained, yet time and time again people who have been helped indicate that listening on the part of the helper is probably the most important asset in rendering assistance.

Accessibility

The trained first-aider who chooses to travel back roads, avoiding main streets where he might see an accident which requires his training, is acting ridiculously.

Just as ridiculous are many marriage partners who possess sufficient training to greatly improve their relationship but make themselves inaccessible by investing an inordinate amount of time in their work, hobbies, church, personal friends, or any number of activities. This lack of accessibility is frequently caused by fear, or the desire to avoid an unpleasant situation, or a lack of love and commitment to one's marriage. We need to learn that growth and repair of the marriage relationship usually involves some discomfort and risk.

Fulfillment

When we help another person treat a physical injury, or else assist our own marital relationship through a committed effort, we receive a fulfillment far beyond any monetary reward.

This fulfillment reinforces our determination to assist people in need. We experience an even greater "high" when we are able to render assistance to and add fullness to our own marriage.

These, then, are the attributes and characteristics required for an effective first-aider. If you don't have them all, they can be developed. Some effort will be required to make yourself an effective first-aider, but the reward you receive from effectively treating a victim of physical injury, or successfully treating your own marriage, far outweighs the cost required.

CHAPTER 6
HOW TO HANDLE ADVERSITY

Adversity is defined as a condition of suffering, destitution, or affliction. Its synonyms are ill-fortune, trouble, or hardship.

Unquestionably, the victim of an accident or sudden illness is experiencing adversity. Likewise, the marriage partners are experiencing serious difficulties in a stagnant or deteriorating relationship.

Handling adversity requires prompt, decisive, knowledgeable action.

After playing in the 1960 College Division NCAA Basketball Tournament, the Wheaton College team bid their coach farewell as they boarded a train in Evansville, Indiana, to travel back to Illinois.

Their coach departed by car over icy roads toward Louisville, Kentucky, to enjoy the Mideast NCAA Regional Tournament.

En route to Kentucky, his car was hit by a motorist who had lost control of his vehicle. Coach's head was severely injured and bleeding profusely. A scoutmaster came on the scene and without hesitation applied pressure to the severed vessels, thus controlling the profuse bleeding. He maintained that pressure for 35 minutes en route to the hospital, until medical authorities could care for the severe lacerations and loss of blood.

As a result of the prompt, decisive, knowledgeable action of this man, Coach today lives a normal, healthy, productive life as the Alumni Executive Director of Wheaton College.

Without this same quality of action, many physical adversities requiring first aid would result in death or permanent injury.

In much the same manner, one must be aware of danger signals appearing in the marriage relationship. Prompt, decisive, knowledgeable action applying proven techniques must be administered in order to sustain the life of the relationship and improve the deteriorating condition.

Once sustained, further steps can be taken to enrich the quality of the relationship.

In first aid and marriage, less serious cases are more easily treated, so one should always be alert to recognize impending trouble in its earliest stages.

Adversity often isn't really accepted; it is tolerated. It is tolerated because those experiencing the adversity feel that when their number is rolled, or when God elects, no action they take can shield them from the approaching ill-fortune.

While that may be true concerning certain types of adversity, the inevitability of other kinds of adversities is certainly open to question.

Surely ill-fortune has befallen all of us from time to time, and some of this has been unavoidable. But adversity also means *hard times and trouble,* and our educated efforts and appropriately planned actions can cause a significant percentage of trouble to bypass our door.

As an example, when we review the yearly statistics showing child deaths due to poisoning, common sense tells us that we need to inventory our entire home and store all poisons in a locked cabinet high out of the reach of children.

Likewise, the fact that almost half of all our marriages end in divorce should encourage us to take preventive measures to insure a continued close relationship in marriage.

Adversity is often claimed as a reason for not attempting to rectify the situation. But when we use adversity in this way it is really just a cop-out. We actually have deeper reasons (which we don't want to share) for not wanting to expend the effort to improve the situation. Not wanting to disclose our true reasons, we expediently claim, "There's nothing we can do when adversity comes."

How often we hear such statements as—

1. "Our marriage was bad from the beginning; why try to change it?"
2. "My wife is impossible; she just doesn't listen. I've given up."
3. "I can't even talk to my daughter now that she's a teenager. There's no use trying."
4. "He looked dead to me when I first saw him by the curb, so naturally I didn't try oral resuscitation."
5. "I hated her from our first meeting and there's no use trying to change my feelings."
6. "Just the feeling I get when I walk in the door makes me not want to go back."
7. "As soon as that kid walked in my class I knew he was trouble."
8. "I don't get a thing out of the Scriptures when I read them, so I'm giving up."

You've heard hundreds of statements fitting this mold, and, if you're like me, you've probably even uttered a few.

In the above cases, are we really astute enough to prejudge the situations and to know that no change will ever occur in spite of our efforts?

Statements such as these are prime examples of adversity which is seemingly accepted but could actually be lessened or even avoided if the speaker was willing to take the necessary steps to improve the situation and possessed the commitment to do so.

Few things are as sad as the dogmatic person who by his statements and actions announces to the world, "I've already made up my mind; don't confuse me with the facts."

When we carefully examine statements 1, 3, and 4, we cam make some pertinent ovservations.

Statement 1—"Our marriage was bad from the beginning; why try to change it?"

If this statement is accepted and no effort is made to remedy the situation, the couple involved are sentencing themselves to a life of misunderstandings, drudging coexistence, and possible marital death.

On the other hand, a mutual effort on the part of husband and wife to improve the situation will very likely result in some improvement, and could well result in a full and rich marriage.

One must honestly answer the question, "Will I be satisfied with a poor marriage or no marriage at all when I have not given my supreme effort to make it exciting and filled with love and mutual blessings?" Remember, *minimum effort will not bring maximum results in any area of life.*

The techniques available to improve your relationship will be thoroughly explained in Chapter 18. You can either appropriate these techniques and attempt to improve the relationship, or else cop out by saying, "What's the use?" and instead continue with your marriage relationship at a level far below the quality God intends for you, your spouse, and your family.

Sentencing your marriage to mere coexistence rather than devoting an all-out effort to achieve fullness is as fruitless as the first-aider in Statement 4 who said, "He looked dead to me when I first saw him by the curb, so naturally I didn't try oral resucitation."

The hasty assumption made by this first-aider, and his unwillingness to become involved with his best effort, could very well have cost the victim his life.

The choice is yours.

One word of caution—the *attitude* with which you help a victim or attempt to improve your relationship will often determine the degree of improvement.

In plain terms, you usually get what you give and expect. A negative attitude—"Well, I'll try it but I'm sure it won't really make a difference"—lacks commitment and will not make any appreciable difference in the status of the victim or the quality of the relationship.

On the other hand, a positive attitude—"I know I can help; let me at it"—shows a real commitment which is likely to produce at least some improvement and very possibly dramatic improvement.

One of the most successful coaches of all time, John Wooden, states that success is "preparing well and exerting your maximum effort to accomplish your task." He then contends that you are successful whether you win or lose because you know you have done your best.

This quality of effort and commitment is what the first-aider owes the victim of an accident or sudden illness, and it is what marriage partners owe their marriage and each other.

38 / First Aid for Marriage

Statement 3—"I can't even talk to my daughter now that she's a teenager; there's no use trying," is certainly a sign of coming adversity.

The choice is yours. Do you really wash your hands as Pilate did in the mock trial of Jesus as if to say, "It's not my fault, there's nothing I can do"? Do you watch passively as the chasm between yourself and your teenage daughter widens and deepens to the point of total noncommunication, or do you discourage adversity by committing yourself to a program which includes learning and unleashing every technique available to you and showing all the love you can toward solving the problem? Remember, minimum effort or no effort will never produce maximum results.

Techniques for Handling Adversity

1. *Recognize early the type of adversity. Then act!* When approaching the victim, a skilled first-aider first checks for serious bleeding and observes if the breathing is regular, after which he or she proceeds to check for other irregularities. Only when you recognize the type of injury can you put your knowledge to work and apply correct treatment.

The marriage relationship must be constantly examined to determine its areas of difficulty, so that proper treatment can be administered. For example, putting a splint on a leg does nothing for arterial bleeding; the victim will die. Likewise, improving sexual techniques in marriage won't do much for the relationship when the real problem is lack of communication. *Early recognition* of problems in first aid or in marriage will result in a higher rate of successful treatment.

2. *Don't accept all adversity.* While some adversities befall us and our families over which we have no control, other adversities can be lessened in intensity or re-routed completely by our committed efforts.

When our child requires first aid because he improperly uses a tool, we take preventive measures by keeping the tool out of his reach or by teaching him how to use it safely and correctly. By this means we often prevent future adversity in this area.

3. *Use adversities to grow.* If communication in our marriage is nonexistent, but we concentrate on learning techniques of communication and applying them in our marriage, communication can actually become the strongest aspect of our marriage. It is similar to the physiological principle of muscle development: when we continue to work a muscle, it thrives and becomes strong, but when we don't use the muscle it atrophies.

4. *Don't dwell on past adversities; don't worry about the past, but concentrate on the future.* Certain adversities over which we have no control, such as a young child becoming ill and dying, are shocking and leave a gaping hole in our completeness at that time.

All authorities agree, however, that dwelling on this adversity for a long duration is mentally and physically unhealthy and unproductive. Certainly we must expect a great deal of sorrow in the ensuing months, but constant dwelling on the loss will prevent us from doing justice to the people who remain and the relationships we have with them.

So it is with adversities in marriage. If they are from the past and you have successfully handled them as a couple, don't dwell on them any longer. You cannot fully participate in the present and future when so much time and effort is being expended by dwelling on the past.

Don't apportion your efforts. It lessens your effectiveness. An acquaintance of mine was becoming disenchanted with his sexual compatibility in marriage. He sought another relationship which consummated in an affair from which he suffered immense guilt.

After a short period he was encouraged to tell his wife of his indiscretion to relieve himself of guilt, even though the risk of divorce was a realistic possibility.

The results were surprising to me. He proudly announced, "she was able to handle it," and proceeded to tell his family and friends how great their relationship was now, while openly discussing his other relationship.

My fears were realized when he recently told me, "Every time we disagree lately she reminds me of that past event, and we have a miserable setback in our relationship."

Don't *dwell* on past adversities. Certainly you will occasionally think about past ill fortune, but *dwelling* on this can only be unproductive.

5. *Learn through adversities.* Although I can write about learning through adversity, practicing this is quite another thing. We never know how we will react until we find ourselves in the circumstances we speak of.

If a victim required first aid because he grabbed a hot wire with high voltage, he will certainly learn through adversity not to make the same mistake again!

Yet time after time our marriage resides in a state of turmoil because we forget the lessons we learned when we rebounded from past adversities.

We seem to learn lessons well when they involve physical injury or death, but we tend to forget the lessons when they involve injury or death to our marriage relationship.

6. *List the circumstances that surrounded the last*

adversity. If that past crisis within your marriage was caused by not communicating, recall those incidents which were prevalent during and just preceding the last crisis, so that when you see them creeping into your relationship again the red light will flash, reminding you to take corrective measures.

7. *Review periodically the measures used successfully during your last adversity, so that you may be able to call upon them again as the need arises.* If your tendency to talk excessively caused your mate to crawl within her shell and lose her identity, and you found a method to control this problem, review the steps taken last time and the symptoms which became evident in your wife when this condition occurred. This acute awareness produced by review will make you ready to pounce on the suffering relationship and make corrections at the earliest appearance of trouble.

Have you ever noticed how much easier it is to handle your second child's first-aid needs? It's usually that way because we have treated those problems before and are now confident that we can handle them again.

8. *Research other ways to successfully handle the adversity.* Don't re-invent the wheel. As you seek to handle a problem and thus enrich your relationship, some of your efforts will be totally unproductive.

But don't quit. Instead, read as much as you can on the subject. Apply those techniques which seem reasonable and appropriate, knowing the limits of what your spouse and you will deem most worthy. Try to select those techniques which seem consistent with your convictions.

9. *Investigate the professionals.* When you find an author whose insights seem keen and whose practical appli-

cations have in the past produced positive changes in your relationship, watch for his new works and be prepared to apply these techniques for ensuing problems. Being on the same wavelength as a knowledgeable author can be of great assistance.

Dr. James Dobson has proven to be this person in our household with his sensitive, practical approaches to discipline and the marriage relationship. We also share his spiritual beliefs and thus feel comfortable with his spiritual insights.

Updating also comes through the professionals. Without reading, one might still be using the "back pressure-armlift" method of artificial respiration rather than the vastly superior oral resuscitation method.

In marriage, why rely on antiquated methods to handle problems simply because they once worked? New research has produced new and improved methods. Read about them!

10. *Recognize that your best efforts fall short of avoiding all adversity.* As we discussed previously, our perceptiveness and skilled efforts can certainly prevent or reduce the seriousness of certain adversities, but others will unexpectedly fall our way no matter what type of action we take.

When this happens, some people suffer great pangs of guilt, as if they were grossly negligent and this is what caused the adversity.

In a great percentage of cases, the serious adversity could not have been avoided by any amount of effort on anyone's part, so guilt is totally uncalled for and only keeps one from resuming previous productivity.

Many people who suffer adversity spend countless hours pondering why it occurred instead of looking ahead to productive times.

11. *Seek out a professional counselor whose convictions are as close as possible to yours.* If you and your spouse were professing atheists and sought professional help for your marital problems, but your counselor suggested that your problems could be partially handled through a conscientious prayer life, your chances of being helped would be about as great as a field mouse surviving a night in a small enclosure with a hungry snake!

You and your mate would likely be so enraged at the suggestion that a quick exit would result. Even if you politely stayed, your efforts would not be focused fully on your problem, and no constructive efforts toward your understanding and solving of the problem would be forthcoming.

And of course the reciprocal of this is also true: a Christian couple should seek out a qualified counselor known to have spiritual depth and insights.

12. *Accept adversity to promote healing.* Doctors say that the attitude of a person who is injured severely is all-important to the healing process. Those wallowing in self-pity usually don't heal as rapidly as the person possessing confidence that he will shortly be fully recovered and back to work.

So it is with an injured relationship. When we wallow in a "woe-is-me" attitude, our chances of effecting a positive change in the relationship are vastly reduced.

Benefits can be derived through adversity, although by open admission we would all rather have the benefits bestowed through some alternate plan. That is not always possible.

When we successfully assist a victim requiring first aid, we derive these benefits:

1. a feeling of satisfaction.

2. a reaffirmation of commitment to human life.
3. increased experienced for future crises.
4. increased self-confidence.
5. increased safety-consciousness.
6. a review of proper procedures.
7. the application of our knowledge and ability.
8. the recognition of a God who cares.
9. an appreciative victim.
10. increased knowledge.

Benefits we receive from handling adversities in our marriage relationships:
1. an improved marriage relationship.
2. a greater appreciation for each other.
3. rekindled love.
4. a keener understanding of each other.
5. increased kindness and consideration.
6. amplified perception.
7. patience.
8. preparedness for the future.
9. a new closeness to God.
10. the ability to assist others experiencing adversity.
11. an increased sensitivity to needs of others.
12. increased knowledge.

Yes, during our lifetime, adversity will most likely affect all of us in our homes, families, and relationships. How well we handle such adversity can determine the extent to which our home, family, and relationship are affected. If we are not prepared to take decisive action based on sound techniques rooted in love, these facets of our lives may be torn apart.

But if handled with constructive responses, the adversity which befalls us can actually add fulfillment to our lives and our relationship.

James 1:2-4 states, "Dear brothers, is your life full of difficulties and temptations? Then be happy, for when the way is rough, your patience has a chance to grow. So let it grow, and don't try to squirm out of your problems. For when your patience is finally in full bloom, then you will be ready for anything, strong in character, full and complete."

I believe the Bible to be the inspired Word of God, and yet I admit that I don't accept all trials with joy and happiness. In fact, sometimes I'm downright perturbed that they have happened to me!

However, I also know that immeasurable joy comes during the trials as I share my sorrows and burdens with Him who created the universe. He supplies peace which cannot be understood, and by His Word He acknowledges the fact that through this trial He is preparing me to better accept and handle future adversity.

What a "high" is produced within me when I realize that the Being who has affected more lives in history than all the world's leaders combined is interested in my marriage relationship and has promised growth through adversity!

CHAPTER 7

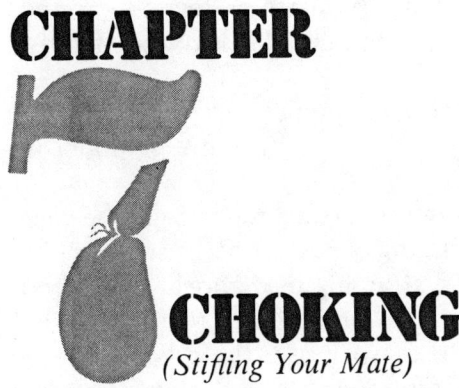

CHOKING
(Stifling Your Mate)

In first-aid terms, choking is defined as a feeling of suffocation, usually caused by an obstruction of the breathing passages.

Symptoms
    Alarming attempts at breathing
    Discoloration
    Discontinued breathing
    Unconsciousness
    Possible death

Treatment
    Remain calm and reassure the victim.
    Remove obstruction, thus opening the breathing passages.
    Administer oral resuscitation.
    Call doctor.

In the marriage relationship, choking can be defined as stifling, smothering, or suppressing.

When one or both marriage partners feel suppressed, the chances of that relationship being healthy and effective are quite remote.

Usually the mate who feels suppressed views the partner as the source of suppression, and the entire relationship is tainted with a feeling of resentment.

When resentment is present, can a relationship be characterized as loving, fulfilling, and mutually satisfying? I think not. At times the relationship may appear to be good, but resentment has a way of periodically rearing its ugly head and exposing the true quality of the relationship.

Suppression and resentment almost always appear together in a relationship. This combination is dangerous, and if triggered it often results in abrupt, ill-calculated action which one later wishes could be retracted.

Recent history provides a beautiful example.

Many marriages existed which coincided with societal expectations. Father departed for work daily in order to support the family while Mother cared for the children and the home.

Those mothers who accepted their role as important and fulfilling were largely unaffected when the women's liberation movement came upon the scene.

However, those mothers who were already feeling suppressed and resentful were spurred into action to denounce their role, arrange for child care, re-enter school, and prepare for their career (which in many cases added to the divorce rolls).

I am not placing a value judgment on the issue of women working, but am rather pointing to a significant fact: suppression and resentment are bedfellows, and unless handled correctly they are capable of destroying a relationship.

Growth in a relationship will rarely occur when one or both partners are filled with resentment due to a deep belief that they will never be able to develop to their fullest potential because of constraints placed upon them by their mate.

A healthy self-concept possessed by both parties contributes much to the success of a relationship.

When suppressed, self-esteem is reduced to rubble as the stifled mate feels that his or her best and most creative thoughts are not worthy of a hearing and have no importance to the welfare of the family. When self-esteem suffers, the relationship suffers proportionally.

The by-products of guilt and stress may also result as the suppressed mate feels that perhaps he or she hasn't mounted best efforts to make worthy contributions to the marriage.

Suppression leads to frustrations, which could ultimately lead to withdrawal of all attempts at communication within the marriage, open rebellion, fighting for equal status, or relief sought through ending the relationship.

None of the above are satisfactory solutions.

Choking (suppression) has no place in a healthy marriage.

A marriage relationship without two vitally involved, contributing, fulfilled partners is about as exciting and stimulating as a three-hour lecture by a nonexpressive, monotone history professor!

Archie Bunker of "All in the Family" frequently roars, "STIFLE YOURSELF, EDITH!"

Next time he does this, observe Edith's facial expression. Is it one of fulfillment and excitement, or is it marked by hurt, lack of self-confidence, resentment, and depression? The answer is obvious.

We may not harshly bellow out "STIFLE YOURSELF" at our partner, but in so many ways we do things daily which have the same disastrous effect upon our mate and therefore adversely affect our relationship.

Following is a list of danger symptoms which could readily indicate that your marriage relationship is in jeopardy of being choked into submission.

The number and frequency of these symptoms appearing in your relationship will indicate the seriousness of the situation.

A few symptoms appearing infrequently contribute to a slow choking process.

Many symptoms appearing regularly indicate that acute choking could be just around the corner.

Your marriage relationship is choking if:

1. You tend to dominate all aspects of the relationship, thus producing a feeling of inferiority and insignificance in your mate.
2. Your spouse feels intimidated by you in the presence of others (rarely speaks and appears nervous or seeks your approval).
3. You demand that your spouse stay at home and care for all household responsibilities while you pursue more fulfilling activities.
4. You answer for your spouse even when the question is directed at him or her. You dominate conversations which involve both of you.
5. You insist on your night out but raise a ruckus when your spouse asks for the same consideration.
6. You demand that your spouse fulfill her role as full-time homemaker even though she wishes a career and feels that it would add to her fulfillment.
7. You discourage your spouse from pursuing a hobby or enrichment-class attendance designed to allow for creativity or recreation.

8. You demand that your spouse account for every hour of the time you are apart.
9. You create guilt by placing rigorous restraints upon your mate, so that he or she feels inadequate to make any independent judgments.
10. You attempt through a variety of means to have your spouse become more dependent on you.
11. You demand involvement in even very insignificant daily decisions—
    a. financially insignificant purchases;
    b. daily minor decisions regarding children.
12. You pursue recreational activities which you alone enjoy.
13. You frequently attend social functions justified as work-related, and leave your spouse at home.
14. You refuse to discuss activities of your day even when requested by your spouse.
15. You are so absorbed in job worries that you have little interest in your spouse or family.
16. You consistently schedule jobs in advance for your mate to accomplish, thus allowing little or no time to accomplish his or her desired tasks.
17. You introduce your mate as "wife" or "husband" only.
18. At a restaurant you order for both of you without acknowledging your mate.
19. You or your mate does not allow friends of the opposite sex.
20. You demand the physical presence of your mate unless he or she seeks your permission and justifies the absence.

21. You allow yourself to be an extrovert at social functions while strongly encouraging "properness and refinement" from your spouse.
22. One mate chooses social activities which both parties will take part in (location of vacations, etc.).
23. You give an "allowance" to your mate while solely controlling the finances.
24. You do not credit your mate for accomplishments.
25. You demand that your mate adopt your religious beliefs and abort his or her personal convictions.
26. You place unreasonable or impractical demands on your mate.
27. You flaunt your superior educational status or intelligence to make your mate feel inferior.

The treatment for "choking" in the marriage relationship is similar to the treatment for physical choking:

1. Remove the obstruction, thus opening the breathing passages.
2. Administer oral resuscitation (help victim breathe)
3. Call a doctor. (Be as calm and reassuring as possible.)

As the first-aider must remove the obstructions from the choking victim to allow him to breathe, so a dominant mate must remove many of the imposed restrictions placed upon the suppressed spouse if the relationship is to be healthy.

Chapter 18 of this book, entitled "Timely Techniques," offers a comprehensive treatment for the majority of marital problems (including choking).

Additional suggestions for treating "choking" within your marriage:

1. Evaluate your relationship.

a. Discuss with your mate what both of you expect and need from your relationship. (Do this periodically, since both of your expectations will change from time to time.) Be honest—don't tell him you want to stay home simply because that's what you believe he wants to hear. Tell him you'd rather work if that is the case. Openly discuss your frustrations.
b. Discuss how what you each expect and need from the relationship differs from what each of you is getting from the relationship.
c. Discuss and formulate a realistic plan (usually involving compromise from both parties) which would constitute a relationship improvement for both parties.
d. Discuss what each of you would be willing to give to achieve the formulated plan. (Know your level of commitment.)
e. Begin working toward accomplishing that plan, realizing that improvement will not be instantaneous but will come only through a consistent effort on the part of both partners.

2. Recognize your mate as a helpmate who possesses an equal investment, and benefits equally by the success of the marriage.
3. Respect your mate and the intelligence he or she possesses. Encourage your mate to actively participate in all conversations while you listen. Compliment and reinforce when nervousness is apparent.
4. Encourage your mate to pursue his or her interests. An excited and involved mate contributes much more to a marriage than a noninvolved, bored mate.
5. If your mate strongly desires a career, encourage its

pursuit. Attempt to assist by facilitating arrangements. If he or she tries a career and fails, succeeds, or quits because of the conflict with other obligations, the fact that you assisted instead of impeded will strengthen your relationship.

6. Encourage your spouse to have some time to himself or herself. Provide assistance in freeing your mate by fulfilling some of his or her obligations. Creativity often comes during unscheduled times, and creativity builds excitement in your mate, and therefore in your marriage.
7. Don't question your spouse (in an accounting way) about every dime spent, or every detail of the day. By not questioning closely, a feeling of trust is fostered and the feeling of confidence as a decision-maker is nurtured.
8. Attempt to foster interests in some hobby or recreational activity. If you can do so, pursue it together, but if not, then pursue them separately. Even if done separately, a new hobby or sport can provide a whole range of new experiences to talk about. The mind and body are renewed through recreation, thus allowing even more energy to be unleashed after participation.
9. Attempt to include your spouse in as many work-related extra functions as possible. He or she should know your colleagues and be somewhat acquainted with your profession.
10. Answer questions about employment in detail from your spouse when an *interest* is shown. Let him or her into your life. If you do, he or she will reciprocate by openly discussing aspects of responsibility previously deemed private.

11. Encourage growth of your spouse. Don't schedule all of his or her free time to accomplish *your* desires.
12. Keep your job in its proper perspective. Don't, by your actions, demonstrate your job's importance as overshadowing your spouse and the relationship you share.
13. Periodically (where practical) assume some of your spouse's duties (especially husbands caring for children and household). This will assist you in appreciating your mate's role and at the same time free your spouse for personal pursuits.

Most importantly, master the techniques discussed in Chapter 18. These techniques, if used regularly, will prevent obstructions from occurring or will remove the obstructions already present, thus allowing life and health to revitalize and enrich your marriage relationship.

Remember: choking or suppressing can lead to the death of a relationship. You must take steps to prevent this tragedy.

CHAPTER 8

FROSTBITE
(Disinterest in Your Mate)

In first-aid terms, frostbite is defined as freezing or partial freezing of some part of the body, usually caused by prolonged exposure to extreme cold.

Symptoms

Pain is sometimes felt early, but subsides later.
Affected parts feel intensely cold and numb.
Victim is frequently unaware of frostbite at first.
Victim becomes mentally confused and impaired in judgment.

As time passes, further symptoms may develop:

Victim staggers.
Eyesight fails.
Victim falls and becomes unconscious.
Shock is evident.
Breathing may cease.
Death may result.

Treatment

Bring victim in from cold.
Protect the frozen area from further injury.
Warm affected area rapidly.
Maintain respiration.

In the marriage relationship, frostbite can be defined as disinterest, indifference, unconcern, insensitivity, or apathy.

One of the most reliable ways of judging the quality of the marriage relationship is by observing the partners together and noting the interest or disinterest they demonstrate toward each other. Although demonstrated interest can be artificial, this interest, if not sincere, cannot be sustained.

If we truly possess an interest in our mate, the marriage relationship has an excellent chance to be effective.

Actions demonstrating indifference toward one's mate indicate that marital priorities must be reexamined.

The cause behind the indifference is extremely important.

Temporary periods of indifference occur in all marriages, and are often dictated by circumstances. The husband who is about to close a financially lucrative sale may be totally devoted to his task for a few weeks, to the detriment of his mate. When the deal closes, hopefully his normal life is resumed and interest in his mate and family will revert to its rightful level.

The pastor whose church is suffering from divisive factions may be totally absorbed in seeking a solution to the problem while neglecting his family during the time of crisis.

Although we all know that our priorities should not be

dependent on circumstances such as these, most of us often fall into this trap.

If these periods of indifference increase in number and duration, or if we must truthfully admit that we're no longer really interested in our mate, our marriage relationship is in danger and definitely needs first aid before death results.

As in the case of physical frostbite, the victim of marriage frostbite is frequently unaware of the problem at first.

Rarely is the "frostbitten relationship" an instantaneous result, but is usually due to a prolonged exposure to extreme cold. In other words, the marriage relationship becomes victimized by the slow and insidious intrusion of unhealthy symptoms wedging themselves between the mates.

Initially, frostbite is painful, but later the pain subsides even though the condition worsens.

Frostbite symptoms in the marriage relationship may at first be a source of discomfort to one or both of the partners. As the symptoms continue, however, the partners may adjust expectations for their marriage downward, thus reducing their pain and frustrations, even though the condition is actually worsening.

Just as an inactive body is more susceptible to frostbite, so an inactive marriage lends itself more readily to relationship frostbite.

When two partners are actively participating in their marriage, they are more alert and more apt to recognize the danger signals warning of impending frostbite.

Below is a list of danger symptoms which could readily indicate that your marriage relationship is entering a state of frostbite which could result in pain or death. The number and frequency of these symptoms in your relationship indicates the seriousness of the problem.

A few symptoms appearing infrequently contribute to a slow, steady cold exposure, while many symptoms appearing regularly indicate acute frostbite and imminent relationship death.

Your marriage relationship is suffering from frostbite if:

1. You are living lives of married singles (basically each living separate lives—he with his chores and friends and she with hers).
2. Your respective interests seem to be yours alone, and the mutual interests you used to share are becoming fewer in number.
3. You notice communication diminishing in time and quality.
4. Affectionate times are becoming more infrequent.
5. Sex seems like a chore or obligation rather than an intimate sharing of love.
6. The frequency of sexual experiences are steadily decreasing (and you're not over eighty).
7. More and more duties are becoming departmentalized:

Her Duties	*His duties*
children	daily job
housework	yard work
transportation of children to events	house repair
art class	dealing with financial matters
church committees	

8. TV time, hobby time, reading time, increases as communication decreases.
9. When together, periods of silence are increasing in frequency and duration.
10. Attempts to talk degenerate to extremes (shouting or silence).
11. Ability to discuss common concerns ceases.
12. The number of independent decisions (even major) increases because both partners know they won't be able to agree.
13. You would rather be alone or with a group because you're uncomfortable alone with your mate due to your inability to communicate with each other.
14. Your mate reads the paper or continues inattentive as you attempt to talk to him or her.
15. The mates know they've wronged each other but won't apologize.
16. You stop performing courtesies for your mate which you formerly did.
17. You truly feel a lack of interest or concern for your mate.
18. You actually feel better and more relaxed when your spouse is not present.
19. You are indifferent to things needed by your spouse.
20. Time between compliments is becoming longer.
21. When together as a family, you talk more to the kids than to each other.
22. At social events you each find yourselves gravitating to other people and spending most of the time apart.
23. You enjoy casual acquaintances more than your mate.

24. You communicate about things and events rather than feelings.
25. You find extra jobs to do so you don't have to be with your mate. (You enjoy your work more than your home life.)
26. Your eye contact during conversation with your mate is diminishing.
27. You avoid contact and touching.
28. When you are honest to your spouse about your feelings, he or she judges your feelings rather than accepting them.
29. You feel lonely and unfulfilled even when together.

The treatment for "frostbite" in the marriage relationship is similar to the treatment for physical frostbite.

1. Bring the victim in from the cold.
2. Protect the frozen area from further injury.
3. Warm the affected area rapidly.
4. Maintain respiration.

As the first-aider must bring the victim in from the cold to allow him to warm and maintain the vital bodily processes, so the disinterested or indifferent spouse must rekindle the lost or dwindling interest and must bring his or her spouse back into the warmth of marital love if the relationship is to be healthy.

Chapter 18 offers a comprehensive treatment for the majority of marital problems.

Additional suggestions for treating "frostbite" within your marriage.

1. *Discuss with your mate whether you both still have a commitment to make your marriage work.* If the

answer is affirmative, renew your commitment to each other and your marriage. For maximum results put the commitment in writing.

This reaffirmation of commitment to your marriage will assist in reinstating your relationship to its proper level of importance.

Some time ago I counseled a mother who was distraught at the low grades earned by her daughter and the seeming inability of her daughter to adjust to our school since her move from the Midwest.

Being a divorcee, the mother allowed her daughter to move out-of-state to rejoin her father and stepmother in an attempt to resolve the situation.

A short time thereafter the mother returned and indicated that the daughter was faltering again, both academically and in the area of citizenship. The mother revealed to me her intention to call her husband and send airfare to retrieve her daughter for another attempt at our school.

The father and stepmother had been concerned enough to have the daughter tested by a psychologist, only to be completely baffled when the results revealed above-normal intelligence with no apparent learning disabilities. When the mother asked my advice, I indicated a belief that her daughter would not show any marked improvement until all adults involved agreed that the daughter would have to choose one location or another and commit herself to success at that school. As long as she could continue without a commitment and bale out to the alternative location whenever problems arose, she would use the escape route more and more frequently, and her achievement would remain inferior.

Upon my advice, the mother retrieved her daughter and indicated that she would be present during grades seven through nine (a three-year commitment). The daughter's grades have risen dramatically, and not one behavior referral has been routed to the office. Even as a commitment to success in school was necessary for this seventh-grader, so a commitment is necessary to your marriage if it is to be marked by success and effectiveness.

2. *Pay attention to your partner.*

After being a football widow for an entire season and experiencing total neglect, one wife had had enough and took matters into her own hands.

As her husband stared intently at the Colts-vs.-Jets game she slipped into the room stark naked and danced between him and the TV, totally blocking his view of the game.

Incensed and surprised, he asked her what was the matter, to which she replied, "Play me or trade me—play me or trade me."

Although this extreme action may never take place in your marriage, many marriages become so cluttered with scheduled events and separate commitments that we totally neglect the person we married.

Redirect your focus toward the one to whom you vowed "I will" at the altar, and practice the communication techniques described in Chapter 18.

This redirected focus will cause your mate to reciprocate and show an interest in your life.

As the mutual interest is rekindled, many of the sexually related symptoms will be eliminated.

Interest and caring creates warmth and a desire to give to your partner, and this gift often encompasses sex.

3. *Evaluate your activities.*

   As marriage and children age, schedules characteristically become more complex. Often the partner's schedules are so cluttered with seemingly valuable events that our partners are all but excluded from our lives.

   In evaluating your present activity schedule, consider the following:

   a. Schedule a daily time with your mate.
   b. Schedule some family activities together when possible.
   c. Learn to say no to some outside requests for your time.
   d. When adding new commitments to an already-demanding schedule, drop a commensurate amount to keep your schedule from becoming too fragmented.
   e. Evaluate each regularly scheduled event in light of its effect upon your relationship. Purge those having a detrimental effect.
   f. Scheduled events should offer variety and should differ in intensity. Some should be light (of the recreational variety). All intensely demanding activities place a strain on any relationship. Don't put yourself into a position of having to decide between a marriage partner and maintaining a hectic schedule of events.

4. *Be polite to your spouse.*

"You always hurt the one you love" conveys a real message. We often tend to abuse and take for granted those who mean the most to us. Maybe we do it because we feel that they're obligated to love us no matter how ugly we act, or perhaps we're burned out from treating outsiders so well. Whatever the reason, it's incongruous with the love we claim to possess for our mate.

When someone talks to us at work we listen, but when our spouse talks to us we nod and continue to read the paper. When our secretary dons a new dress we never miss telling her how stunning she looks, but when our wife looks exquisite she often goes unnoticed.

Abuses could be cited at length, but it's up to *you* to reverse the trend.

Isn't it logical that the person you've chosen to share your life with should receive the ultimate in courtesy, justified compliments, and consideration?

Try it! Set the paper down and look her in the eye when she speaks. Ask her questions about her statements to let her know you're interested.

Compliment her when justified. Open her car door as you used to when you were courting her.

Let me assure you that you will receive more than the effort extended in being considerate toward the one you love.

5. *Let your children grow.*

Frostbite can be worsened by a mate focusing almost exclusively upon children to the exclusion of his or her mate.

When two people fall in love and marry, God intended that those two stay together until separated by death.

As children come into the marriage, love should be shown to the children and felt from both parents.

As the child grows and matures, a healthy independence is normal. If the parents recognize this need and grant increasing independence in love, the child will develop normally.

"If either parent clings and smothers a child when love and freedom should be shown, the child begins to experience the loss of his warmth and spontaneity, which is the beautiful quality of an emotionally healthy child. Such a child thus becomes self-conscious. Feeling manipulated, his or her tendency is to respond by trying to manipulate."*

Much is written about the detrimental effect upon the child involved, but little is written about the effect upon the spouse whose rightful place has been usurped by the maturing child who wants to gain release from the domineering parent.

Seek as a couple to grant increasing independence to your child as warranted, and reinvest the time and attention released in each other as marriage partners. The benefits derived will be many.

6. *Rediscover the characteristics in your mate which originally attracted you to him or her.*

Often years of marriage tend to amplify the irritants and diminish the strengths present in our spouse. A periodic assessment of our spouse's strengths and positive characteristics may well reveal that all of

---

*From page 41 of *The Gift of Inner Healing*, by Ruth Carter Stapleton, © 1976. Used by permission of Word Books, Publisher, Waco, Texas.

them which originally attracted us are still present, plus many other strengths developed through the years.

This awareness will allow us to appreciate our spouse and his or her commitment to us.

By nature many people are negatively oriented. Focusing on strengths places our relationship in the proper perspective.

Remember: frostbite, if not treated, can lead to the death of a relationship. Steps must be taken to treat this emergency in order to allow the relationship to thrive.

CHAPTER 9

BURNS
(Downgrading Your Mate)

A burn is an injury that results from heat, chemical agents, or radiation. It may vary in depth, size, and severity, causing injury to the cells in the affected area.

Burns are classified as follows:

1. First-Degree Burns

Symptoms

    Redness
    Mild swelling and pain
    Rapid healing

Treatment

    Apply cold water applications or submerge burned area in cold water.
    Apply dressing if necessary.

70 / First Aid for Marriage

2. Second-Degree Burns

Symptoms
    More painful
    Greater depth of tissue damage
    Red appearance
    Blisters
    Considerable swelling
    Plasma keeps surface wet-appearing

Treatment
    Immerse burned part in cold water.
    Blot dry.
    Apply sterile bandage.

3. Third-Degree Burns

Symptoms
    Deep tissue destruction
    White or charred appearance
    Complete loss of all layers of skin

Treatment
    Cover burns with thick sterile dressing.
    Keep feet or legs elevated if they are burned.
    Watch for breathing difficulty.
    Get victim to hospital.

The marriage relationship often suffers from burn injuries as real to the partners as painful physical burns are to the victims of excessive heat.

Burns in the marriage relationship are defined as injuries to either or both of the partners which result from varying degrees of downgrading by their spouse.

The depth of the burn suffered depends upon the severity, frequency, and duration of the downgrading incidents.

Burns in the marriage relationship are classified as follows:

1. First-Degree Burns

Putting down your mate's actions, ideas, suggestions, feelings, or contributions (sometimes subtly, sometimes harshly).

2. Second-Degree Burns

Putting down your mate (the actual person or personality) in a critical manner.

3. Third-Degree Burns

Putting down your mate or his actions in a personally degrading manner.

It should be noted that a burn of lesser degree can become a burn of maximum severity if the attack on your mate's actions switches to an attack on your mate, or if the degrading process begins.

It should also be noted that even as most physical burns are accidental, most burns within the marriage relationship also begin accidentally, even though their continuance may not fall into this same category.

As physical burns leave scarred tissue, burns in the marriage relationship also leave scars, though most of these are internal.

One of the biggest problems associated with physical burns is the danger of secondary infection. In marriage, damage from burns can create a similar atmosphere, greatly increasing the susceptibility of the relationship to other problems and complications.

Physical burns are often unnoticeable at first, but show up some time later. Likewise, burns in the marriage may seem to have no immediate effect on the relationship, but later become evident in the form of hostility, transference, or other associated symptoms.

Whether or not the mate is present and witnesses the downgrading doesn't determine the degree of burn.

The circumstances surrounding the burn can complicate matters greatly, and usually affect the type of first aid required to successfully treat the marriage relationship.

As an example:

If the downgrading is incurred in *private*, even though severe it can usually be handled exclusively by the partners involved.

If the same downgrading of one's mate occurs in *public*, the presence of other people will increase the complexity and severity of the problem, since other factors are now involved. However, the first aid for this kind of burn will not necessarily involve other people outside the marriage relationship.

There is a proper time and place to give constructive criticism, but giving criticism in public is a departure from common sense and will usually result in nothing but strife.

Constructive criticism is at times necessary if the integrity of the relationship is to be maintained, but it must be carefully controlled.

A fire can be beautiful, functional, and romantic when confined to a fireplace on a cold winter night, but totally destructive as it whips through your house uncontrolled.

When we put too many logs on the fire the heat becomes intense and unbearable, and the observers move away due to excessive heat. Similarly, you cannot put too much constructive criticism on a person even if you mean well.

Uncontrolled fire is a frightening destructive force, and criticism (even if intended as constructive) is like the fire. Just as the fire can be either constructive or destructive, so criticism is capable of being either constructive and helping or else destructive and destroying.

Rules for Criticism

1. Choose the proper time and location for administering criticism.
2. Don't administer criticism in large doses even if you mean well.
3. Don't use highly flammable fuel products. (Don't criticize areas your mate is extremely sensitive about unless both are in the proper mental state to mutually agree to do so.)
4. Don't awfulize:
   Don't generalize by saying, "You always ......" or "You never ......" This usually burns deeply and requires extensive treatment.
5. Since many persons receiving criticism become defensive, be prepared to receive criticism about yourself. This is your golden opportunity to set an example of accepting criticism in a mature and constructive manner.

Read carefully the symptoms which follow. Note the fact that they are grouped into categories of first-degree burns, second-degree burns, and third-degree burns.

Examine your marriage relationship in light of these danger symptoms. The greater the number of these symptoms in your relationship, and the more frequently they occur, the greater your need to administer first aid to your marriage relationship.

If the symptoms continue unchecked, the relationship may be terminated in death, much like a severely burned victim who received no first aid or medical treatment.

First-Degree Burns in the Marriage Relationship

Symptoms—You are burning your mate if:
1. Your mate's ideas, although expressed, are rarely considered as a basis for action.
2. When your mate makes a suggestion, it is received with a condescending attitude or action (all-knowing smile, smirk).
3. You often express amusement at your mate's attempts to contribute.
4. You often explain why your mate's suggestion is not logical.
5. Even when your mate's ideas are acceptable, you must still modify them to remind him or her of your superiority.
6. Sometimes you ignore your mate's comments completely, with no comment or recognition.
7. You rarely solicit your mate's opinion, no matter how important the matter or how much it affects both of you.
8. You openly denounce your mate's contributions by offhanded comments, such as "Forget it."
9. You have a tendency to label your mate's ideas as stupid or unrealistic.
10. You take sole credit for ideas which work out well, but attribute ideas which fail to your mate.
11. You dominate the conversation when your spouse is in the presence of other people, thus disallowing his or her contributions.

12. You compare your spouse's ideas to some standard deemed as foolish: "Your ideas are as dumb as Watergate."
13. You commonly make cutting jokes about your spouse. (Although humorous, these often convey your true feeling.)
14. You direct insulting comments or questions toward your spouse:
    "If I want something done right I might as well do it myself."
    "Can't you ever think something through and make the right decision?"
    "Please try to act appropriately, will you?"

Second-Degree Burns in the Marriage Relationship

Symptoms—You are inflicting second-degree burns to your mate if:

1. You make statements directed at your spouse such as:
   "No honest person could do that."
   "How could you be so naive as to believe that?"
   "That's just the way you are."
   "You can't even tell a joke."
2. You indicate to your mate that you and you alone will make the decisions in the family.
3. By your actions you demonstrate that your mate is below you in status, ability, and intelligence.
4. You take the best and leave what's left to your mate—you take the Lincoln, she the V.W., you take the choice piece of meat, she the less desirable.
5. You intensely question your mate on decisions made or a course of action chosen.

6. You question your mate's capabilities of even applying for a job considered as an advancement.
7. You correct your mate while he or she is telling an anecdote or relating an experience.
8. You comment to your mate, "Now that you're 40 years old I'm gonna trade you in on two 20's," thereby creating questions about your mate's desirability.
9. You comment on the attractiveness of others, particularly those exhibiting characteristics which your mate may lack.

Third-Degree Burns in the Marriage Relationship

Symptoms—You are inflicting third-degree burns on your mate if:
1. You call your mate derogatory names.
2. You direct profanity or vulgarity at your mate.
3. You insult your mate by attacking his or her qualifications.
4. You attack the intelligence and capabilities of your mate. ("It's surprising you can even hold a job.")
5. You openly comment on your mate's shortcomings to outsiders, causing them to have a lower opinion of your mate.
6. You use your mate as the butt of jokes.
7. You rarely speak a kind word about or compliment your mate.
8. You put down your mate in front of children, relatives, or close friends.
9. By your actions you indicate the worthlessness of your mate.

10. You discuss problems between you and your mate outside marriage, always making your mate appear wrong.
12. You express anger at your mate with no apology.
13. You introduce your mate by saying, "Here's my wife, she's only a housewife," or "Here's my husband, he's only a janitor."
14. You denounce, through humor, your mate's qualifications—"Are you kidding? A bank teller? She can't even keep our checking account straight!"
15. You make statements which:
    a. Lower your mate's status in the view of others.
    b. Take honor from your mate.
    c. Deprive your mate of his or her true function.
    d. Reduce your mate's desirability.
    e. Reduce your mate's stability.
    f. Reduce your mate's respectability.

Similarities exist between the first-aid treatment for physical burns and the treatment required to alleviate the suffering caused by burns in the marriage relationship.

The treatment for physical burns at any level involves removing the source of excessive heat and cooling the injured site.

The treatment of burns within the marriage relationship requires similar action. To be effective, the treatment must remove the source of downgrading, and the injury must be allowed to cool.

Chapter 18 of this book presents techniques which, if employed and mastered, will allow burns within the marriage relationship to become a rarity.

A few additional treatment suggestions are included here which deal specifically with treating burns.

Treating Burns Within the Marriage Relationship

1. *Recognize the worth of your mate.*

   "Two heads are better than one" is frequently stated but seldom practiced.

   Marriage is a complex institution requiring skill and effort if success is to be achieved. A marriage provides the opportunity to enlist a helpmate to provide input into the difficult decisions regarding employment, child-rearing, education, spiritual development, and future plans.

   Certainly a person who views his or her spouse as inferior can make all the decisions on his own, but I guarantee that three outcomes will result.

   a. *The decisions will be inferior to what they could be.* Ignoring input from a mate who views things from a different perspective and emotional base is shortchanging the entire marriage relationship.

   b. *The decisions will not be supported wholeheartedly.* As a school principal I can attest that I receive nearly unanimous support for decisions I make in which the teachers have provided input. The same is true of the marriage relationship. A wife having a decision imposed on her without having a chance to provide input will support the decision far less enthusiastically than if her involvement has been solicited.

   c. *The self-concept of the noninvolved person will suffer, and his or her contributions to the marriage will be lessened appreciably.* Your mate can easily perceive whether you view him or her as a valuable contributing member to the marriage.

   If your actions indicate his or her nonimportance

(i.e., by not soliciting input) to the relationship, his or her efforts to contribute will decrease.

Hopefully your decision to marry involved respect for your mate's abilities and intelligence as well as his or her charms. Think of the *worthy* attributes which attracted you originally. These attributes probably still exist and may even be stronger now, but are clouded by kids, responsibilities, and a hectic schedule. Look through the complexity of everyday life and simply appreciate again the worthy individual you married, embracing him or her as a helpmate and equal contributor to marital success.

2. *Respect your mate's ability to contribute.*

   Healthy relationships often involve disagreements. Disagreements if discussed openly and frankly can contribute to the effectiveness of the marriage relationship.

   However, when disagreements always seem to end by one mate deciding to do what he or she deems best, without ever incorporating contributions from the other mate, the relationship needs a working over.

   Mates must respect each other's abilities to contribute if a healthy relationship is to result.

3. *Review the capabilities and strengths of your mate periodically.*

   Although the grass may appear greener elsewhere, a review of your spouse's strengths and capabilities often creates a renewed appreciation for him or her.

   This appreciation can result in reduction or elimination of the "putting-down" tendency which creeps into many marriage relationships.

4. *Review the goals and priorities for your relationship.*

This process requires input from both partners, followed by mutual agreement on goals and priorities.

Working through this process will demonstrate anew the satisfaction derived by two contributing members focusing their combined efforts on one task.

As priorities are established for goals, couples will often be struck with the fact that achievement depends on their combined effort and may result in renewed teamwork.

This achievement cannot occur when either partner is the object of downgrading.

5. *Evaluate love in your relationship and see if it coincides with God's definition of love.*

Read First Corinthians chapter 13 to reacquaint yourself with the attributes of love.

a. *"Love is very patient and kind."*

Putting down or degrading is not in the vocabulary of a lover.

b. *"Love is never boastful or proud."*

Having your own way at the expense of your mate demonstrates an unhealthy pride; true love doesn't allow this.

c. *"Love is never selfish or rude."*

Downgrading one's mate or degrading through rudeness is a flagrant transgression against God's definition of love.

d. *"Love does not demand its own way."*

Real love seeks to incorporate the strengths and feelings of one's mate in decision-making and in bettering the overall marriage relationship. When one mate demands his or her own way, the effectiveness of the entire relationship is lessened.

e. *"If you love someone, you will be loyal to him no matter what the cost."*

Loyalty involves support and honesty. Differences should be discussed frankly but should not affect one mate's support for the other. Love mandates defense of and support for your mate regardless of the circumstances.

Loyalty and defense presupposes respect for your mate.

f. *"You will always believe in him, always expect the best of him, and always stand your ground in defending him."*

Even when circumstances create doubts in your mind concerning your mate's actions, love demands that you expect the best of him, believe in him, and defend him or her against all foes.

Downgrading your mate directly contradicts this truth.

If this "love evaluation" reveals that love has been ousted from its rightful place in your marriage relationship, you must develop plans for rearranging your priorities. A weekend at a good marriage seminar will allow you as a couple to reexamine your proper marriage priorities and to renew your commitment to each other and to Christ.

6. *Examine feelings which result when you are put down. Periodically review these.*

Put yourself in your mate's position; think of the last time you were put down, and reflect on the feelings which were created in you.

If you are able to recall these feelings and personalize them, you will have more appreciation and empathy for your mate and will avidly avoid taking action which might put him or her in that position.

7. *Guard against oversensitivity.*

    Few people would enjoy a relationship devoid of humor; a new dimension is added to a relationship in which both partners can laugh with each other and at themselves at times.

    Some partners consider the slightest quip directed at them a personal put-down. They then overreact, creating a gulf between them and their mates.

    Accept these quips as they are intended; let them add to rather than detract from the quality of your marriage.

    However, when humor is consistently directed toward your mate in a destructive way, reaction in love is merited, and discussion must follow.

    There are some people, however, who delight in being miserable. Be sure that you don't search for reasons to find dissatisfaction with your mate, for when you search carefully you will always find them.

    Enjoy the strengths and goodness of your mate, and expect the best from him or her.

8. *Don't reciprocate.*

    I'm often amused as I watch two adult drivers approaching each other at night, and one fails to dim his bright lights after repeated signals.

    Frequently the perturbed driver, now being blinded by the bright lights, strikes out by switching his brights on and equally blinding the other driver.

    The drivers pass each other partially blinded at 60

miles per hour, thus greatly increasing the chances of a head-on collision.

Often marriage partners react similarly. One partner puts down his mate, who, instead of taking appropriate action, lashes out and puts down her mate, thus greatly increasing the chances of a head-on collision.

The quality of first-aid treatment administered to the marriage relationship must be commensurate with the degree of destruction caused by detrimental behavior.

If the putting-down process has been severe and regular in occurrence, the techniques in Chapter 18 should be administered faithfully.

If the application of such techniques over an extended period fails to produce an effective cure, professional counseling should be sought, since *extensive burns may require admission to the burn center.*

Above all, the most real danger existing when a mate is consistently put down is the danger that the put-down mate might choose to live up to the put-down reputation, thus contributing to the relationship only at that level.

As an educator I can cite numerous examples which clearly illustrate that a student who is told consistently that he or she is nothing but a troublemaker soon becomes just that.

In a recent experiment in my school, I instructed my assistant principals to send congratulatory letters to the parents of some of our troublemakers who had demonstrated even a bare minimum of improvement in their behavior, complimenting them and their parents on progress made.

Not to my surprise, the next semester was marked by a conspicuous absence of these students from the discipline roles!

Expect the best from your mate, and that's what you'll receive!

9. *Don't cover the burn unless temporarily necessary.*

Although some physical burns (depending upon their severity) need to be covered by a sterile dressing, the best healing takes place when the burn is exposed to air and light.

When the danger of infection has passed, the burn is uncovered to increase the rapidity of healing.

In the marriage relationship, burns should not be covered up and internalized. Internalization (harboring within) produces many detrimental side effects, further affecting the marriage relationship.

Although at times it is necessary to temporarily avoid dealing with severe burns (for example, when both partners are highly charged emotionally), the burns will have to be treated in the near future in order for the marriage to progress toward fullness.

Chapter 18 fully discusses techniques for effectively treating these burns.

CHAPTER 10

EYE INJURY
(Inability to View Your Relationship Clearly)

In first-aid terms, "eye injury" is defined as an injury caused (usually) by a foreign object in the eye which has an irritating effect and the potential of scratching the surface of the eye, thus causing further injury.

Symptoms
  Redness of eyes
  Burning sensation
  Pain
  Headache
  Overproduction of tears
  Blurred or unclear vision

Treatment
  Do not rub.
  Wash hands.
  Remove object.
  Do not remove with sharp utensil.
  Flush eye with water.
  Visit doctor.

A physical eye injury can be extremely painful, although most eye injuries heal very rapidly.

The common symptom produced by almost all eye injuries is the inability to view situations clearly, as they really exist.

In the marriage relationship, "eye injury" can be defined as intense emotional involvement resulting in the inability to view your relationship clearly.

Physically, injury to the eye can be caused by a variety of means. A hard blow, flying debris, sun exposure, a sharp object, or a serious illness may all be direct or indirect causes of eye injury and the associated inaccurate perceptions.

In the marriage relationship, "eye injury" and the associated inability to accurately view our relationship is usually caused by intense negative emotional involvement. The causes of these injuries may also be many, and may involve thoughtless acts, thoughtless deeds, or oversensitivity on the part of both or either mate.

From childhood most of us have been cautioned to "count to 10" when we are angry. This technique concludes that we can react more rationally when we refrain from reacting until the intense emotion has had an opportunity to subside and we can see the situation clearly.

Reacting hastily when we are emotionally upset often involves overreaction and increased complications. I have read of a victim of a rattlesnake bite who overreacted in fear, and in an attempt to cut himself with a razor (to allow the blood to carry the venom from his body) did so too deeply and severed an artery. He bled to death.

In the marriage relationship, it is wise indeed to refrain from immediate important responses or decisions while you are in the negative emotional state of anger, fear, despair, sadness, or disgust.

As an example, a spouse who has just suffered the loss of his mate and finds himself in a strong state of depression should be encouraged to refrain from making important decisions regarding his future until some healing has taken place and the intense depression has somewhat lessened, allowing him to view his overall situation clearly.

Most strong emotions make it difficult to accurately assess a situation, think clearly, or solve a problem. Valuable mental energy needed to perform these tasks is drained or diverted by emotion.

Many a marriage has ended tragically when one or both partners have eye injuries (blurred vision), and, without treatment or time to heal, make inaccurate and unfounded statements or act thoughtlessly, thereby compounding the problem. Fatigue can also affect one's ability to focus accurately on relationship problems.

The following is a list of danger symptoms which could readily indicate that your marriage relationship is suffering from eye injury.

The number and frequency of these symptoms appearing in your relationship will indicate the seriousness of the situation.

A few symptoms occurring infrequently will have a lesser effect upon your marriage than many symptoms appearing frequently. The latter could result in relationship termination.

Your marriage relationship is victimized by eye injury and blurred vision if:

1. Encounters with your mate frequently leave you depressed (often more depressed than the circumstances warrant).

2. Encounters with your mate frequently result in anger (often more angered than circumstances warrant).
3. Circumstances currently causing these strong emotions are less intense than formerly were required to evoke the same response.
4. The emotional state triggered by your spouse lasts a longer period of time than such states formerly did.
5. Your emotional eruption is directed at your mate rather than the incident which caused it.
6. You often lash out at your mate and after the smoke clears feel the necessity of apologizing.
7. You act hastily and emotionally and then feel compelled to retrace your steps and alter your previous actions because you see them as irrational.
8. Your body is reacting unfavorably to the stress produced by your frequent emotional upheavals (e.g., headaches, ulcers, nervousness, etc.)
9. You are aware of the areas of concern regarding your spouse's actions but still cannot refrain from reacting violently when they occur.
10. Something bothers you greatly about your mate and causes you to see red, yet you hesitate to talk to him or her about it.
11. Your mate is attempting to change a habit which bothers you, but you focus harshly on his or her occasional failure, thus causing a negative response in him or her.
12. You react to pressures (e.g., employment pressures or out-of-town guests about to visit) by lashing out at your mate and reacting to trivial things in an emotional manner; your mate becomes the victim of displaced hostility.

13. You lose your peripheral vision and tend to focus on the narrow or selective problems in marriage; you don't see all the related aspects of the total picture. In this situation you tend to amplify the faults of your mate and the weakness of your relationship and focus on them excessively while overlooking all the benefits and good points of your mate and marriage.
14. You do things which you know infuriate your mate, such as minimizing his or her concerns, or labeling him or her as "silly," or tuning him or her out when you disagree with a point of view.
15. You do things to make your mate jealous, such as flirting with members of the opposite sex.
16. You partake in activities which frustrate your mate, such as withholding sex in an attempt to gain favors (for example, chores around the house).
17. You are dishonest with your mate. If you are dishonest and your mate discovers this, he or she may think you are dishonest in many areas of your relationship. This affects the clarity with which he or she sees you.

The treatment for eye injury in marriage is similar to the treatment for physical eye injury.

The main treatment for both consists of removing the foreign object or source of irritation in a safe and sanitary manner.

Once the cause or source of eye irritation is removed from the eye, the rapid healing process usually begins.

Likewise, as the stimulus causing the negative emotional state in marriage is removed, the healing process begins.

Chapter 18 offers a comprehensive plan to prevent or treat most marital problems.

Additional suggestions for treating "eye injuries" within your marriage:

1. Identify the irritant. Discuss with your mate the specific irritants which are responsible for evoking your strong negative emotional feelings (for example, clothes on the floor, procrastination, impoliteness, flirtatious behavior). Your mate dislikes these emotional states and the resultant problems as much as you do, so be honest with yourself.

    You cannot remove an irritant completely unless you identify it completely. Don't say, "Your negative attitude bothers me" when you really mean, "In the last three days, most comments you've made to me have been negative." Provide specific examples.

2. Resolve to remove the irritant. Once it is identified, ask your mate to assist you in handling the problem by refraining from introducing the irritant.

    Make certain that your mate realizes that the total problem is not caused by him or her alone. Be honest and acknowledge that your sensitivity is part of the problem.

3. Develop alternatives together. It is difficult to stop a habit without a plan, and a *shared* plan has an even greater chance of success.

    If you are asking your husband to remember to record a written check in the checkbook (irritant) so that an accurate checking account can be maintained, you may offer a plan which encourages him to simply scratch the amount of the check on a slip of paper and drop it on the dresser at night as he empties his pockets.

4. Evaluate the irritants. Even if your spouse refuses to change, is your continued reaction to the irritant

worth the possible termination of your relationship? You may have to face this question.
5. Chart the frequency of your emotional eruptions. For a reasonable duration of time, such as one month, log the frequency of emotional eruptions occurring and specify the irritants which caused them.

   The number may be very revealing. If it is large, work to reduce the frequency over a reasonable time period. Set a goal, such as a 50 percent reduction in one month.

   If your determined efforts result in a reduction to the level of your goal, reward yourself with a predetermined reward. If your efforts do not result in a reduction, consider professional counseling. Where both partners are determined to reduce the frequency of their negative behavior, they should exchange mutual rewards when their goals are met (for example, dinner out together).
6. Ask your spouse to tell you truthfully when your behavior is about to evoke an emotional eruption in his or her behavior.
7. If you are fatigued, recognize that fatigue often causes blurred vision and distortion of reality. Try to postpone any hard-and-fast statements or irrational decisions until morning, when you're fresh and emotionally cool.

If your spouse is the emotional one:

1. Respond in love or not at all until the intensity of his or her emotional state subsides.

   Responding in like manner will only intensify your spouse's state of emotional upheaval and will increase the length of the unproductive period. Responding harshly keeps pressure on your mate, and pressure builds intensity. Calmness, on the other hand, alleviates intensity.

2. Recognize what you did to cause the emotional state.

   As you become more aware that a certain action you perform evokes an emotional state, don't demand your rights but seek to terminate that action, thus removing the irritant. This sacrifice is certainly worth it if the relationship is improved.

3. Apologize in love that your irritant contributed to the problem.

   The emotional spouse will likely feel guilty for the irrational behavior, so your apology, if sincere, will somewhat alleviate the burden.

4. Avoid talking about highly sensitive areas to which your spouse reacts violently until both of you are prepared to talk about these areas, and then do so in a calm and emotionally uninvolved manner.

5. Attempt to develop more tolerance for your mate's habits which seem to evoke the strong emotional responses within you. Look at the issues and determine if you should be as sensitive to that issue as you really are.

6. Realize that what we see and perceive in our marriage is highly correlated with brain functions and is interpreted and evaluated through our value system. All we see is evaluated in accordance with our value system.

Physically, it is important to have our vision tested regularly. In marriage, many tools exist to evaluate our clear perception, and vision should be tested in marriage as well. The communication techniques described in subsequent chapters will serve as a test to determine whether or not your marriage is viewed accurately, with keen perception. Use these techniques to avoid permanent damage to your marriage relationship as a result of eye injury.

CHAPTER 1

SHOCK
(Withdrawal or Failure to Respond)

In first-aid terms, "shock" is a condition resulting from a depressed state of many vital body functions, a depression that could threaten life even though the victim's injuries would not otherwise be fatal.

Symptoms
    Skin is pale, cold, and clammy.
    Pulse is rapid.
    Breathing is shallow, rapid, or irregular.
    Injured person is frightened, restless, apprehensive, or comatose.

Treatment
    Keep patient lying down.
    Loosen patient's clothing.
    Get patient to hospital.

Physical shock is usually caused by a trauma of some form to the body. A serious injury, fracture, burn, infection, heart attack, stroke, plus additional conditions may cause one to enter the state of shock.

When the trauma first occurs, the body enters this state as a protection in an attempt to withdraw into itself (e.g., when one cuts himself deeply, circulation is slowed through shock so that bleeding from the open wound is somewhat reduced in intensity).

While shock is the attempt of the body to protect itself by "drawing in," shock can become self-destructive. Shock can kill even when the victim's injuries are not fatal.

In the marriage relationship, shock is the tendency to withdraw or not respond to problems or situations as a result of a traumatic occurrence in the relationship.

Serious injuries to the relationship, such as fears, mistrust, jealousy, unfaithfulness, disrespect, and others may cause one or both partners to withdraw for protection into a state of shock.

Withdrawing may originally feel good and offer temporary solace, but continuing to operate in this withdrawn state becomes self-destructive and will lead to the death of the relationship.

In these traumatic situations, the individual is so overwhelmed by the problem or situation that he or she does not respond at all, or else responds abnormally. Often one or both mates are hurt in the marriage, but instead of facing the problem they simply withdraw and back off. In effect, they become noncommital, almost like spectators watching the relationship, and in this state they fail to deal with the critical situations which may eventually kill the marriage.

Depending on the seriousness of the incidents involved, shock may be temporary and fleeting or it may be secondary and spell impending disaster.

Following is a list of danger symptoms that could readily indicate that your marriage relationship is in jeopardy of being threatened by shock. The number and frequency of these symptoms appearing in your relationship will indicate just how serious the situation is. Many symptoms appearing regularly in your relationship indicate that acute shock and therefore death could be just around the corner.

Your marriage relationship is approaching or already is in the state of shock if:

1. Either mate knows the incidents which cause him or her to withdraw, but instead of dealing with them through discussion, attempts to suppress them.
2. When situations occur which are deeply bothersome to you or your mate, instead of discussing them with loving concern you retreat to your spot in front of the TV, or to your hobby, or to the garage to work on the car. Or else you might jog for an hour or pull out work from the office. In short, you do anything to avoid confronting the problem.
3. You retire earlier and earlier, using sleep as an escape mechanism to avoid discussing the problem.
4. More and more things which your mate does bother you, but you handle them through silence or withdrawal.
5. One or both mates greet certain bothersome situations with statements or actions denoting finality, thus eliminating the possibility of meaningful discussion:
    a. packing your suitcase as if you're going to leave.
    b. verbally threatening to leave.
    c. telling the kids you're going to split up, and

asking them to denote who they're going to be loyal to.
6. Your comfort seems more important to you than dealing with situations you know have to be faced.
7. Instead of talking out bothersome situations, you react by calling your mate a name or hollering "Shut up." This sets up a climate whereby you have no alternative other than to be silent.
8. You walk away, stating one of the universal withdrawal phrases:
   a. "I don't even want to talk about it."
   b. "I can never, ever talk to you about anything."
9. You threaten to go home to Mom, or you actually pack and leave.
10. Each bothersome circumstance results in you crying. Subconsciously you are withdrawing from discussing the situation by claiming weakness.
11. You physically assault your mate. This guarantees withdrawal and nondiscussion.
12. Displeasing situations involving your mate are handled by withholding pleasantries from him or her, such as sex.
13. You are driving your mate toward shock when you are aware which of your reactions will cause him or her to withdraw and still choose to do them. (For example, your mate is very jealous, yet you continually flirt in his or her presence, knowing that this will cause him or her to withdraw into silence and eliminate all communication.)

Treating shock in marriage is not dissimilar from treating physical shock. In both marriage and medicine, the situation causing shock must be found out and alleviated.

In addition, drugs are occasionally administered to shock the body back from withdrawal to action. Drugs are not necessary to bring the marriage out of shock, but other stimulants are. While Chapter 18 of this book contains many techniques which will allow you to avoid or handle shock within your marriage relationship, I offer the following additional suggestions for treatment of shock:

1. Realistically examine how much success is usually achieved toward solution of a problem when one or both of you are nonresponsive.
2. Examine the additional detrimental effects which occur when a problem is handled by withdrawing. Not only is the problem avoided, but it is usually further complicated through inattention. Additional doubts are raised in the minds of both mates, and absence of discussion eliminates all possibility of uncovering the misunderstanding which may have caused the original hurt.
3. As drugs are sometimes induced to bring a victim suffering from physical shock back to action, the following stimulants can be used to bring a marriage partner out of shock:
   a. *Warmth and relaxation*
      To bring a victim of physical shock out of shock, the victim is laid down and covered. In the marriage relationship, the mate suffering from shock should be basked in the warmth of your love and allowed some time to relax and reflect with you about the situation which has transpired. Often spending some time together will allow you and your mate to rekindle the love and understanding which previously existed.

b. *Communication techniques*

Withdrawal is usually a sign that the marriage partners have never mastered communication techniques. Once you have communicated well, you realize that withdrawal is an inadequate method of handling the situation. These techniques are covered thoroughly in Chapter 18. Once you experience good communication within the marital relationship, both partners realize that communication is necessary in the solution of any problem.

Remember, if shock exists within your relationship you should know how to handle it. If not handled properly, shock can end the marital relationship.

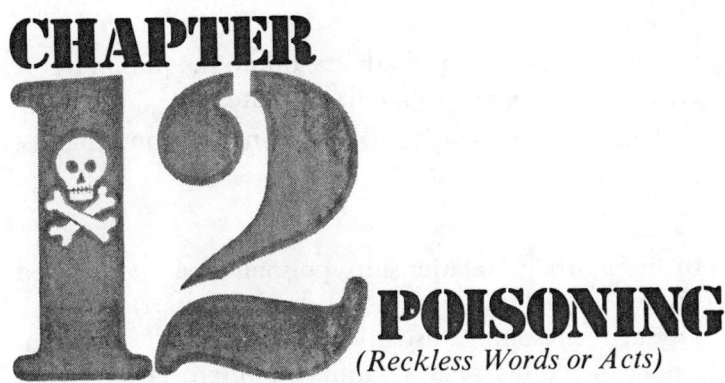

CHAPTER 12 POISONING
(Reckless Words or Acts)

In first-aid terms, a poison is defined as any substance that tends to impair health or cause death when introduced into the body or onto the skin surface.

Symptoms

Symptoms of poisoning vary greatly. Aids in determining whether a victim has swallowed poison include:

Information from the victim or from an observer
The presence of a container known to contain poison
The condition of the victim (sudden onset of pain or illness)
Burns around the lips or mouth
Breath odor
Abnormal size of the pupils of the eyes
Unconsciousness

Treatment

1. Administer the antidote recommended on the container from which the poison came.

Call your doctor or poison control center immediately.

If you can't get medical advice, dilute the poison by giving several glasses of milk or water.

If the type of poison is unknown, induce vomiting.

In the marriage relationship, poisoning can be defined as careless or reckless remarks or deeds in marriage.

Physical poisoning usually involves small children. Poisoning in the marriage relationship often starts when a couple is first married and becomes a habitual pattern for the remaining married years.

Physical poisoning most often occurs due to carelessness. The parents did not put the container of poison out of their child's reach, or a person did not check the label carefully before ingesting the substance in the container. A little more thought, a little more time, and the tragedy or near-death could have been averted.

Poisoning in marriage also stems from carelessness. One lashes out with a reckless remark. One does something without considering his or her mate. This poisoning can become habitual, with the same circumstances evoking the same careless remarks or action time after time.

After one's careless actions have led to the physical poisoning of a child, he usually takes considerable caution to see that all possible prevention is exercised from that date forward. In our marriage relationship, however, poisoning seems to occur over and over without preventive steps being taken.

Poisoning in the marriage relationship may be motivated by the conscious or unconscious desire to strike out in a pressure situation with the intent of retaliating toward one's mate. Often the mate who is the victim of poisoning is truly unaware of his or her actions which are causing this retribution.

This type of reckless and cruel behavior within the marriage relationship is cumulative, similar to the roentgens received when X-rays are taken. Execessive X-rays within too short a period may cause cancer and physical death. Excessive reckless and cruel remarks or actions in the marriage relationship are cumulative and may produce the same disastrous consequences.

If allowed to continue, these abuses become the accepted pattern and seem to be evoked regularly in certain situations; one mate starts depending on these abuses to settle scores with his or her mate.

Frequently the reckless remarks or actions are focused on the mate's sensitive areas or personal characteristics.

Each careless statement made or reckless action taken further drives a wedge between partners, but love attempts to draw the partners back together again. Repeated remarks or actions (wedges) break the couple completely apart, to the point that love eventually can't bridge the chasm. Soon the partner who is a victim of this poisoning believes that he or she truly is what his or her mate says.

The ultimate fatal dose of poison enters the marriage relationship when the remarks become public knowledge.

One of the most detrimental aspects of the entire poisoning process is that it lowers the self-esteem and self-concept of the victim. When your mate believes that he or she is unworthy, that is how he or she will contribute to the marriage relationship. This shortchanges both the victim and the mate.

The following is a list of danger symptoms which could readily indicate that poisoning is taking place within your marriage relationship. Before this poisoning becomes cumulative and your marriage relationship ends fatally, be aware that *your marriage relationship is being poisoned if:*

1. Reckless remarks, similar to those below, are frequently made:
   "I wish you'd leave."
   "We'd be better off without you."
   "Cleaning house is your job. Don't ask me for help."
   "I'll spend my money; I earn it. You spend yours."
   "Why don't you leave?"
   "I don't know if I even love you anyway."
   "I don't know how I ever got hooked up with you."
   "I should have married someone rich."
2. Often the reckless remarks are focused on your mate's sensitive areas. For example, if he feels she is not satisfied with the amount of money he earns, your reckless remarks may constantly bring this to his attention. If her physical appearance is not what she would like it to be, your comments in pressure situations are directed toward this sensitive area. If he is considerably older than you, you may make disparaging remarks from time to time about his age. If she lacks athletic ability and cannot come close to hitting a tennis ball over the net, you may continually refer to her as a "klutz." If he lacks mechanical ability and can hardly put a nut on a bolt, you make discouraging remarks about his mechanical ability as you pay the Sears repairman.
3. You often brag or rave about the mates of others who can do the things you wish your mate could do.
4. When depreciating remarks do not garner the proper response, you try them out on friends and acquaint-

ances. This greatly intensifies the feeling of resentment on the part of your mate.
5. You find that your mate tunes you out more frequently so that he or she does not have to listen to the sensitive areas of concern.
6. Often this tuning-out is generalized. In addition to not listening to your reckless or careless remarks, your mate tunes you out completely and doesn't even hear the *constructive* things you might say.

The first-aid treatment for poisoning involves administering an antidote to neutralize the poison.

Such is also the case in the marriage relationship. The person who victimizes his mate through reckless or careless remarks and actions must find an antidote to neutralize these destructive situations in an attempt to heal the hurt created within the marriage.

In addition to those detailed techniques for administering first aid to your marriage found in Chapter 18, the following suggestions are offered for treating poisoning within your marriage.

1. Recognize that when you issue a reckless statement or take part in reckless actions, you never improve a relationship. Focusing on a person's sensitive areas usually causes the party involved to become defensive and unwilling to discuss the situation.
2. Take special note of your mate's reaction after you abuse him or her. Is it one of openness and a desire to discuss the situation, or is it one of anger or silence?
3. Identify the situations which seem to compel you to take this thoughtless and careless course of action.
4. While noninvolved emotionally, list preferable constructive ways to handle the situation without depreciating your mate or children.

5. Ask your mate to assist you by identifying the remarks or actions which hurt him or her and affect a willingness to communicate.
6. Recognize the fact that striking out at your mate through actions or thoughtless words demonstrates personal weakness and frustration on your part.
7. Realize that poisoning can be controlled. It is not an inherited weakness but a habit which through conscious effort and desire can be eliminated.
8. Seek divine assistance. Pray to your Creator for strength and wisdom in eliminating this destructive factor of your relationship.

CHAPTER 13
DRUG ABUSE
(Foreign Substances)

In first-aid terms, drug abuse is the excessive or persistent use of a drug without regard to accepted medical practice.

Symptoms
- Increased or decreased physical activity through action on the central nervous system
- Increased or decreased heart rate
- Increased blood pressure
- Increased body temperature
- Dilated or enlarged pupils
- Flushed face
- Partial loss of emotional control

Treatment
- Check to see that an open airway exists.
- Give oral resuscitation if necessary.
- Maintain body temperature.
- Get the victim to a hospital or physician as soon as possible.

Often drugs assist us. Administered properly, drugs often have a miraculous effect in relieving pain and suffering, combating disease, and saving life. When the same drugs are abused, however, they become enemies.

It is a commonly accepted fact that medical doctors prefer that you not take drugs unless absolutely necessary. The human body has a tendency to develop dependence on drugs, and it often requires increased amounts of the drug to produce the same result after the body has developed a tolerance toward it.

It is better to maintain your health through exercise, wholesome diet, and generally good health habits than to bail yourself out of a problem with drugs.

In the marriage relationship, the use of drugs can be defined as introducing modes of thought, philosophy, or techniques previously untried in the marriage in an attempt to improve the relationship.

Often these new practices divert one's attention from the real problem at hand, and therefore complicate the situation rather than clarify or solve it. Recently a number of techniques have been encouraged by professional counselors in the hopes that these would improve personal health as well as one's marriage relationship.

Couples experiencing problems in their marriage have been encouraged to jump headlong into such things as:

1. Open marriage, in which they are free to carry on a relationship with various members of the opposite sex while maintaining their own marriage.
2. Sensitivity encounters, in which people bare their souls and discuss all the intimate details of their lives and feelings with virtual strangers, clothed or unclothed.
3. Occultic studies.

Drug Abuse / 109

4. Transcendental meditation, which purports to provide serenity and satisfaction through meditating.
5. EST—Eberhard Seminar Training—which, if practiced successfully, supposedly allows one to picture oneself floating serenely above one's problems.
6. Reading pornographic books which graphically describe great sexual detail. This supposedly allows one to free oneself from his or her inhibitions, thus allowing greater sexual satisfaction in marriage.

I am certainly not opposed to new techniques which actually better one's marital relationship (any more than I would oppose a new miracle drug that effectively treats cancer or some other dreaded disease), but I would caution you that even though *some* of these new techniques offer help to some people by improving relationships, many techniques detract from the real problem and instead become a false focus of the couple's attention and energies.

When this occurs, the root of the problem is not dealt with at all, and the problem continues or even grows more complex. Several cautions apply to using drugs in your physical body or introducing new practices into your marriage.

1. Use drugs only when necessary. Correspondingly, don't search for new techniques to use in your marriage if your marriage is already fulfilled.
2. Examine each drug to see that it is tried, tested, and approved. Use the same caution with marital techniques; use only those practices and techniques which have been tested by time and proven successful. You need not jump at every new practice you hear of in order to be the first couple on your block to try it.
3. Avoid instant wonder drugs that claim to cure all. In

your marriage avoid new techniques which make tremendous claims of rectifying all problems. Unless your case is terminal, there is no need to panic and grab wonder drugs.

4. Take specific drugs only for the malady for which they are intended. Use the same principle in marriage; use only those techniques which are designed to assist with the particular problem which is currently evident in your marriage. In marriage we sometimes hear of a new technique and sign up immediately for a weekend crash course without even knowing if the technique is designed to remedy our particular problem.

5. When you find a good drug, don't overindulge in it. If you do, you will build up a tolerance to it, and it will lose its effectiveness. The same is true in marriage. If you have found a new communication technique which seems to work in your marriage, don't use it to the exclusion of other techniques. In so doing you may overlook other vitally important tasks which need to be accomplished.

6. Make certain that the new techniques or practices are consistent with your convictions. While aspirin is certainly an approved drug for Christians, marijuana or barbituates are probably not within Christian convictions. A Christian husband experiencing sexual problems would not normally employ a surrogate wife (a popular trend among some marriage partners in the secular world) in order to increase his sexual capabilities, since the problem is likely to be further complicated through guilt acquired from knowing he had violated a law of God.

If the new techniques seem to be practical and meet the

Drug Abuse / 111

tests as outlined above, don't hesitate to try them, but in so doing be certain to abandon them if, after fair trial, they fail to improve your marital situation. If you continue using them, even though they fail to correct the situation, you may become addicted. Addiction, whether to drugs or marital techniques, is always an unproductive activity.

CHAPTER 14

HEART ATTACK
(Blockages to Keep from Exposing the Real You)

In physical terms, heart attack usually involves a blockage in one of the blood vessels that supply the heart. A heart attack may or may not be accompanied by loss of consciousness. If the attack is severe the victim may die suddenly. The degree of pain is not always a good indication of the seriousness of the disease.

Symptoms
1. Persistent chest pain
2. Gasping and shortness of breath
3. Bluish discoloration of lips, skin, and fingernails
4. Extreme prostration
5. Shock, as a rule
6. Swelling of the ankles

Treatment
1. Make the victim comfortable.
2. Provide ventilation.
3. Begin artificial respiration if the victim is not breathing.

4. Have someone call for an ambulance.
5. If the victim has helpful medications available, help him take them.
6. Do not give liquids if the victim is unconscious.
7. Do not attempt to transport the victim until you get medical advice.

In the marriage relationship, heart attack may be defined as blockages which keep your mate from knowing or seeing the real you.

Some couples have been married for years and yet know each other only on the surface; they have built virtual walls around themselves.

Marriage encounter weekends have provided a successful way for thousands of couples to learn how to tear down these walls, block by block, through learning effective communication techniques and skills which allow the sharing and acceptance of each other's feelings.

Nothing is more beautiful than to observe a couple whose relationship is increasing in love and understanding as these walls, once set in concrete, are dismantled block by block and the partners begin to know and accept each other with full exposure of each other's strengths and weaknesses.

Many of today's young couples considering marriage are taking advantage of premarital counseling which teaches communication skills designed to prevent the construction of these walls or blockages.

Only when you have true openness and acceptance of each other in marriage do you achieve the level of fulfillment that God intended marriage to have.

The following is a list of danger symptoms which could indicate that your marriage relationship is in jeopardy of suffering from a heart attack. The number and frequency of these symptoms occurring in your relationship will indicate the seriousness of the situation. In our physical body, once a complete blockage occurs, a heart attack is imminent and death may ensue. In the marriage relationship, blockages can be just as disastrous.

Your marriage relationship could suffer from a heart attack if:

1. You attempt to avoid situations in which the real you and your feelings might be exposed. You may avoid these situations by:
   a. changing the subject to a safer, less threatening topic.
   b. responding at a completely different level.
   c. counterattacking.
   d. using defense mechanisms, such as anger or any variety of means. (For example, when your wife broaches the sensitive area of the excessive time you spend in job-related activities, you fly off the handle in anger rather than openly discussing the reasons for the situation. When you wish to talk about the infrequency of sex in your marriage and the lack of sexual fulfillment, your wife says, "That's your problem," or starts talking about problems related with the kids in order to avoid this unpleasant, sensitive topic.)
2. You wear a variety of masks to cover your real feelings, since feelings expose the real you. This is done for fear that the real you might not be accepted. The masks show a fictitious you which you feel might be more readily accepted.
3. You make a concerted effort to sidestep the issues which will cause a display of emotions. If you're

angered, or seen crying, you view this as a sign of weakness.
4. You frequently talk about surface issues so you won't have to face real issues. For example, you talk about the weather and current events, but you rarely discuss feeling-level issues with your mate. You use the out, "That's your problem, not mine," when your mate starts talking about areas that are dangerous territory as far as you are concerned. Throwing the problem at your mate provides safety for you.
5. You feel tired and unproductive, since you spend much energy in building walls to protect yourself, and therefore a lessened amount of time can be spent on constructive pursuits.
6. You fear you might be hurt through exposure if people know the real you. You fear that people will continue to peck at your weaknesses like chickens peck at an exposed sore on a fellow chicken.
7. You find yourself bothered by inner tension and the feeling that you could almost explode. Inwardly you want to let off steam by sharing your inner feelings with someone.
8. You may feel the need to exercise in an attempt to work off this tension, but it will not help nearly as much as discussing those inner deep feelings with your spouse.
9. You feel embarrassed or guilty after those few times you've shared deeply, as though you've exposed too much of yourself.
10. You thrust yourself headlong into your work or other pursuits which involve great blocks of time, so that free time is not left for your spouse to pursue uncomfortable territory.

11. You receive inadequate love and understanding because you forget that a wall has two sides: it may protect you from danger and exposure, but it also blocks you from receiving understanding and strength in times of weakness, comfort when troubled, and caring when you have a feeling of non-acceptance.
12. You experience fear, which keeps you from seeing other issues around you clearly.
13. You even shield yourself from God at times. You pray on the surface rather than sharing your innermost feelings. This is ironic, since if you believe in God you certainly believe in His omnipotence, which allows Him to know everything you're thinking or feeling. This dishonesty with God may actually affect your relationship with Him. You feel stress and tension and even develop physical problems such as headaches or ulcers, since these are perpetuated by your fear of being found out or exposed.
14. You occasionally don't know why you've just experienced an episode of anger or intense emotion. Often this occurs in an attempt to derail your spouse as he or she zeros in on a touchy area. This is your way of saying, "Stay away—you're near my threshold of tolerance."
15. You increase the frequency of the techniques in order to avoid exposure of yourself. As you continue to find safety in avoidance, this cycle turns into a habitual unhealthy state.

As does a first-aider who treats a person with a heart attack, you must make the victim feel comfortable, provide good ventilation, and see that he or she is breathing. This treatment is similar to what we must do in our marriage to prevent heart attack from tearing it apart.

Chapter 18, entitled "Timely Techniques," offers a comprehensive treatment for the majority of marital problems.

Additional suggestions for treating "heart attack" within your marriage:

1. Recognize the fact that emotions and feelings are never wrong, but instead add depth to you as a person and are accepted by those who are your true friends.
2. Be aware that comfort which comes from building walls around us not only protects us but also prevents us from receiving such needs as love, acceptance, and understanding.
3. Intimately share yourself with your spouse. You may experience a "high" from this sharing which you have never experienced before, and this in itself may be what is needed to begin the sharing process in your marriage.
4. Try to determine what masks you are wearing, and carefully employ the techniques described in Chapter 18 in order to unmask yourself. This will give you a feeling of honesty and acceptance, and will also reveal to you that you do not have to pretend to be something else in order to be accepted.
5. Attend a marriage encounter weekend to learn and experience in a controlled environment the skill and deep satisfaction you receive while sharing yourself and your inner feelings with the one you love.
6. Recognize that sharing only a surface you and not the real you is selling yourself and your mate short, since

it is being dishonest and preventing your relationship from growing.
7. Share the experience and satisfaction you received through letting yourself be just you with your spouse. Often the embarrassment you think you'll feel (for example, when you cry as a man) will not be felt and will be viewed by others as a sign of strength.
8. Be honest with God. He knows your thoughts and inner feelings already. Read Keith Miller's book *A Taste of New Wine*.
9. Recognize that openness about your vulnerability really shows strength. A decade ago a man who did the dishes was considered relatively feminine, but now a husband who plunges into the housework and assists his wife with household activities is considered secure about his manhood.
10. You will soon see that when you share your innermost feelings with other people, they reciprocate by sharing their feelings with you, which adds to the depth and trust in the relationship.
11. Seek to learn new skills to bypass the blockage you have created to protect your sensitive and critical areas. By learning these new skills you will regain access to the person you love.
12. Heart patients often have to diet in order to control further buildup and blockage in the vessels. You, too, should be aware that you can reduce junk, such as fear and insecurity, from building up and preventing communication in your marriage. You have control over many of these detrimental factors.
13. Pacemakers are often implanted to increase the function of a damaged heart through stimulation. Correspondingly, marriages once affected may need

added stimulation to recover and operate smoothly. This stimulation may be in the form of counseling, marriage encounter, and just working out new approaches with your mate to stimulate both of you and to break your present routine.

14. Physical exercise is necessary to prevent the blockage of vessels to the heart. Exercise is also necessary in marriage. The continual art of sharing feelings and setting time aside for this is discussed thoroughly in Chapter 18. This is exercise which will prevent heart attack in your marriage.

Remember, true physical health involves clear, uninterrupted flow of blood to the heart. Marriage also requires clear, uninterrupted communication and sharing between the partners.

Physically, some heart defects can be present at birth. Similarly, some marriages are not soundly based on love at their inception. Even in these cases, love can grow and techniques of communication and sharing feelings can be part of this growth. In effect, these will contribute toward a rehabilitation program.

Remember, nothing is more fulfilling than to share yourself and be accepted as you really are, with all your strengths and weaknesses.

CHAPTER 15
DROWNING
(Wallowing in Self-Pity)

In first-aid terms, drowning is defined as suffocation by submersion in water.

Symptoms
Victim is not breathing.
The victim's tongue, lips, and fingernails have become blue.
There is a loss of consciousness.
The pupils have become dilated.

Treatment
Clear the airway first.
Begin mouth-to-mouth resuscitation.

In the marriage relationship, drowning can be defined as one or both members of the marriage relationship wallowing in self-pity. As water can suffocate a victim in drowning, self-pity can lead to the death of a marriage.

We have all been around people who feel sorry for themselves. If you're like me, you can take just so much of this type of person without heading for higher ground. It is very difficult to take a steady diet of the "woe-is-me" attitude.

For some reason, certain people seem to delight in being miserable. They're miserable if the weather is sunny because we haven't had enough rain. They're miserable if it's raining because it really would be nice for summer to be here. They're miserable if it's cold because we need warmer weather. They're miserable if it's too hot because it costs money to run the air conditioner. They're miserable if they're stuck at home because they just never get a chance to go anywhere. They're miserable when they're on vacation because there just isn't anyplace like home.

I'm always happy to be able to leave a person who wallows in self-pity and has an extremely pessimistic attitude about almost everything.

However, many people are married to such a person. My deepest sympathy is extended to them.

There is a tendency for the negative person to influence others around him (or her). As a principal of a secondary school, when I hire young teachers all full of new ideas and enthusiasm, I try to steer them to mature teachers who are positive in their outlook. Occasionally, a first-year teacher will be influenced by a negative teacher, and soon his attitude and performance are affected.

Since a person with tendencies toward self-pity affects so many other people, it is imperative that this situation be corrected in order to permit a healthy, productive family life.

The following is a list of danger symptoms which could readily indicate that your marriage relationship is in danger of drowning. A few of these symptoms occurring from time to time may be relatively normal. Many of these symptoms occurring frequently indicate that immediate first aid is necessary if the marriage relationship is going to survive.

Your marriage relationship is drowning if:

1. Statements like the following are common in your marriage:
   "You just don't understand me. No one does."
   "You and the kids are against me."
   "You kids must not love me."
   "Your actions sure don't say you love me."
2. One partner uses the technique of sulking in order to gain consideration for his or her viewpoint.
3. Your mate frequently cries as a result of being questioned about decisions or issues.
4. One partner makes irrational decisions when in a state of self-pity. Self-pity causes one mate to resist assistance from the other mate. As in the case of physical drowning, the panicking victim often tries to fight the one who is assisting him or her. This panic causes an overreaction to trivial situations.
5. Whenever things don't work out to your advantage, you claim that others have been unfair. (For example, you don't receive the new job, and therefore the boss played favorites.)
6. The self-pity you wallow in produces guilt in your partner.
7. Your partner tries hard to appease you in an attempt to relieve your feeling of sorrow, and in so doing violates his or her convictions.
8. When your mate's efforts to appease you don't lift you from wallowing in self-pity, he or she becomes frustrated and is possessed with feelings of inadequacy. This may make him or her evaluate the worth of the efforts and of the marriage itself.
9. You claim you'd like to get away and be by yourself,

but you rarely do because you need the presence of others to feel sorry for you.
10. You delight in wearing your feelings on your sleeve. No one ever has to guess your mood, for it's very obvious just by looking at you. You love to be asked, "What's wrong?" and usually respond, "Oh, nothing," when all the time you look as if a truck has hit you.
11. An entire group of people has just been through the circumstances which are responsible for your current self-pity, yet you feel that the effect on you is much greater than the effect on the other people.
12. At times you talk of suicide, but you aren't really serious, for suicide would discontinue the pity of other people.
13. You rarely see the good in any situation, but instead tend to dwell on the negative.
14. You blow statements completely out of proportion and don't take them at face value.
15. When your mate says to you, "I really don't like that shirt on you," you hear, "She really doesn't love me." When you say to your wife, "Boy, the house is sure dirty," or "I don't really care for that dress," she interprets it as "He really doesn't love me."

The person obsessed with self-pity always expects the worst. In fact, sometimes he or she actively recruits things to feel bad about. He or she overreacts to the first sign of discomfort. A gas pain is assumed to be cancer.

The wife who is a victim of self-pity believes that her husband is involved in an affair if he simply mentions a person of the opposite sex who is attractive. In addition to feeling that her mate doesn't care about her, she also generalizes and feels that others around her don't care either. The self-pitier sometimes pictures a conspiracy between her mate and others against her.

If carried to the ultimate without any help, the victim of self-pity becomes paranoid.

There are few things that are more destructive to a marriage than one of the partners wallowing continually in self-pity. One thing worse, however, is when *both* partners pity themselves.

When only one partner is a victim, the positive attitude of the other can often offset the detrimental effects. But with two partners feeling sorry for themselves and their plight, an unhealthy parasitic cycle is created. Chapter 18 of this book offers a comprehensive guide for the treatment of most such marital problems.

Additional suggestions for treating "drowning" within your marriage:

1. Observe a negative person who is filled with self-pity as objectively as you can. Determine what you think of that person, and whether or not you enjoy being around him or her.
2. Recognize that your purpose in self-pity constitutes an attempt to have your own way and is really used as a substitute for skills that you do not possess.
3. Determine whether being emotionally upset is productive and ever clarifies the issue or strengthens your relationship.
4. Note the expressions and responses around you when you wallow in self-pity. Do they display love and understanding, or do they show an element of disgust for your immaturity?
5. Realize that you can have control over this facet of

your life, and can eliminate self-pity through the acquisition of proper skills.

6. Note that much energy is used in seeking self-pity, and that when this energy is used in such an unproductive pursuit it lessens your available energy for productive pursuits.
7. Keep a record of the number of times you use self-pity in your marriage, and the reasons you feel you must use it. Note the frequency over a specified period of time. Duplicate that specified period of time and attempt to reduce by 50 percent the frequency of using self-pity. If you're successful, reward yourself. Notify your spouse of your attempts, and allow him or her to help you with this constructive pursuit.
8. When you're tempted to seek self-pity, realistically appraise the worst possible consequences which could occur if you simply dealt with the situation without using this behavior mechanism.
9. Examine your needs. Are they really being met when you seek self-pity?
10. After you seek self-pity, note the increased complexity of the situation you've just attempted to alter.
11. Seek divine assistance. Pray that you will not use that detrimental behavior mechanism again.
12. Prioritize your values. Is honesty, integrity, and self-esteem important? If it is, certainly self-pity will be dropped, since it tries to achieve ends through dishonest means.

Drowning can lead to the death of a relationship, but you can prevent the drowning.

CHAPTER 16

HEAT EXHAUSTION
(When You've Got No More to Give)

Physical heat exhaustion occurs when the intake of water is inadequate to compensate for the loss of fluids through perspiration.

Symptoms
    Approximately normal temperature
    Weakness and fatigue
    Headache; perhaps cramps
    Pale and clammy skin
    Profuse perspiration
    Nausea
    Possible fainting

Treatment
    Give victim sips of water.
    Lay victim down.
    Loosen restrictive clothing.
    Provide cool environment.
    Take victim to hospital.
    Keep victim home from work.

We can mistakenly assume that exhaustion in the marriage relationship occurs only in marriages which have been in existence for many years. Such is not the case.

I'm sure you have witnessed marriages at 50-plus years in which both partners are enthusiastically and energetically contributing to the vitality of their relationship.

And I'm sure you've also observed partners in a relatively new marriage already characterized by total exhaustion and a corresponding lack of contributions to their relationship.

We can become victims of physical exhaustion when we tax ourselves heavily, regardless of our age.

Exhaustion in the marriage relationship is likewise no respecter of age.

We enter the state of heat exhaustion when we lose more water than we take in. We enter the state of matrimonial exhaustion when we are continually required to contribute more to maintaining our marriage than we believe we derive from our marriage.

In many marriages, only one mate is suffering from the symptoms of marital exhaustion, although in some marriages both mates suffer from the same malady.

Fortunately, the physical body possesses amazing rejuvenation capabilities, and in most cases the victim of physical exhaustion can operate at full capacity again in a short time. The same can be true in most marriages. Marital exhaustion can be temporary; the partners, if they handle the situation correctly, may soon resume their former contributing mode.

Although marital exhaustion may pass, proper recognition of the symptoms and proper application of the correct treatment are important if marital fullness is ever again to be achieved.

The following is a list of the danger symptoms which

could readily indicate that your marriage relationship is in jeopardy of dying from exhaustion.

The number and frequency of these symptoms appearing in your relationship will indicate the seriousness of the situation.

A few symptoms appearing infrequently contribute to a slow, steady exhaustion pattern.

Many symptoms occurring regularly indicate that marital death from exhaustion may be lurking nearby.

Your marriage relationship is approaching the state of exhaustion if:

1. You feel you've given all you can possibly give and are still experiencing marital strife or lack of fulfillment.
2. You no longer attempt to solve problems in your marriage, even though you're aware of them.
3. You find yourself glossing over problems you previously deemed as vitally important.
4. You feel that living your convictions in marriage is no longer really worth the effort.
5. The criteria most important in determining whether you'll take action is, "How much effort will it take?"
6. You no longer explore new frontiers together.
7. You no longer seek new ways to add fullness to your marriage.
8. You handle similar situations the same way year after year; you are satisfied with the status quo, never seeking new and creative approaches.
9. You choose inactivity, rejecting activity involving your mate because of all the trouble and work.
10. You choose staying home in preference to activities

involving your mate which could add to your marriage.
11. You frequently think about how long you've been married.
12. You more frequently find yourself not saying anything (responding less and enjoying it more).

As in the treatment for physical heat exhaustion, the victim must lie down and rest comfortably, temporarily free from the burdens of everyday life. In marriage, the spouse suffering from exhaustion must temporarily cease his or her efforts while evaluating the marriage relationship.

Most of us have experienced the feeling of trying to produce even though we are physically and mentally exhausted. What a fruitless feeling exists when we, with clouded mind and exhausted body, see our productivity drastically falling off! In situations like these, it is much better to back off, get some rest, and attack the situation anew with an alert mind and responsive body.

Chapter 18 details many techniques which will reduce the chances of exhaustion occurring in your marriage and will allow you to effectively treat the symptoms already present.

Additional suggestions for treatment are:

1. Evaluate the alternatives open to you. When you're exhausted you may either:
    a. quit or change.
    b. rest, then attack the problems with renewed vigor.
    c. evaluate whether you can afford to be exhausted and thereby have a stagnant or deteriorated relationship.

Examining the three options, most people prefer to

spend their energies attempting to improve their existing relationship.

2. Evaluate the source of your exhaustion.

   Sometimes we are guilty of spinning our wheels excessively without contributing anything. All efforts should be directed at a well-understood goal.

   At times, great energies are being expended and wasted performing certain tasks within our marriage which are directed inappropriately and contribute little but exhaustion to the marital partners. One is reminded of a hamster aimlessly rotating the wheel in its cage, but making absolutely no progress.

3. List the time expended in making your marriage successful.

   You may find that even though you thought you put much time and effort into your marriage, you actually put in very little.

4. Talk to your mate and determine the priorities you two have for your marriage. Adjust your efforts accordingly. Maybe rather than hitting the top twelve priorities, you should expend your energy on the two or three things which are now your top priorities. Remember, as the relationship grows, priorities change. The astute couple is continually reevaluating their priorities so that their efforts are directed appropriately for their benefit.

5. Honestly examine the effects of not facing problems due to exhaustion. Most people can readily attest that problems, if not faced for whatever reason, become more complex and require more energy than would originally have been required.

6. Reflect on those past situations which remain the same because you expended no effort to change

them. Could you really accept that same feeling again, knowing that the situation might have been improved through effort on your part?
7. Examine the impact of nonactivity. Physically, when a muscle is not used it atrophies and becomes almost useless. Correspondingly, to have a vital marriage the marriage must be active. If it is not active, the marriage isn't vital. Unless you strive to make your marriage successful, it will wallow in mediocrity.
8. Step back, relax, and take a fresh look. If everything is in proper perspective, you will see that frequently your marriage still offers much. Set new goals for that marriage, realizing that you will never achieve your maximum potential toward marital fulfillment without goals. As a couple, you will never know your potential if you don't expose yourselves to new challenges.

Remember, heat exhaustion can lead to the death of your marital relationship. You must take steps to prevent this from occurring.

CHAPTER 17
CHECK YOUR FIRST-AID KIT

The following instructions exist in the Reader's Digest Association First Aid Booklet.*

First-Aid Kit

Assemble your first-aid supplies *now*, before you need them. Don't add these items to the jumble of toothpaste and bobby pins in the medicine cabinet. Instead, assemble them in a suitably labeled box (such as a fishing-tackle box or small tool chest with hinged cover), so that everything will be handy when needed. Label everything in the kit clearly, and indicate what it is used for. Put in a copy of this guide.

Be sure not to lock the box—otherwise you may be hunting for the key when seconds count. Place the box on a shelf beyond the reach of small children. Check it periodically to restock used items.

---

*Reprinted with permission from the "Reader's Digest Handbook of First Aid." ©1975 The Reader's Digest Association, Inc.

Checklist of Supplies

(All items are obtainable without prescription)

Sterile gauze dressings, 4 x 4 inches, individually wrapped, for cleaning and covering wounds

Roll of gauze bandage, two inches wide, for bandaging sterile dressings over wounds, etc.

Box of assorted adhesive dressings (Band-Aid, Curad or similar products)

Roll of inch-wide adhesive tape

Roll of absorbent cotton

Pint bottle of sterile saline solution (one level teaspoonful of salt to one pint of boiled water)

Mild antiseptic for minor wounds (consult your druggist)

Tube of petroleum jelly

Bottle of calamine lotion, for sunburn, insect bites, rashes, etc.

Bottle of ipecac syrup to induce vomiting

Container of powdered, activated charcoal to absorb swallowed poisons

Box of baking soda (bicarbonate of soda)

Small bottle of aromatic spirits of ammonia

Pair of scissors

Pair of tweezers

Packet of needles

Sharp knife or packet of stiff-backed razor blades

Medicine (eye) dropper

Measuring cup

Oral thermometer

Rectal thermometer
Hot-water bottle
Ice bag
Box of wooden safety matches
Flashlight

Note the suggestion, "Assemble the supplies before you need them." Certainly the loss of precious time while groping for makeshift supplies can impede your efforts and have detrimental effects on the victim.

Even a well-stocked first-aid kit doesn't make you well. You can die right next to it if it is not applied or if the person using it is ignorant of proper first-aid methods.

"Put a copy of this guide in your kit." A guide will be necessary in some emergencies, so have it handy. Only those people who know the manual and its techniques through continued review or practice will be able to work confidently without the resource book at hand.

"All of the supplies are obtainable without prescription" means that there is no excuse for not being prepared for the emergencies with supplies intact. You can't blame your druggist or doctor, for you alone must accept responsibility.

What a great correlation with the marriage relationship!

1. Is your marriage "first-aid kit" ready now, even if you think you don't need it?
2. Do you have a resource guide contained in the kit ready to supply the answers when you need them?
3. All the necessary supplies are obtainable without great cost and without permission from outside sources.

Checklist of Supplies

1. The techniques outlined in detail in Chapter 18 should be practiced and learned. If you keep them in your mind through continual practice, they will become a part of your marriage relationship.
2. Your Bible should be used as a manual. It touches on every subject imaginable which relates to your marriage and its effectiveness.
3. Excellent reference books are available which amplify and explain many techniques found successful in treatment of problems within marriages.
4. Exercise the power of prayer with your mate. The Scriptures say, "Where two or three are gathered together, there I am in the midst." Claim this promise and many other promises within the Scriptures to assist you and your mate in achieving marital success.
5. Fellowship with other couples; observe the strengths evident in their marriage, and learn from them.

You are now ready for emergencies which will come along from time to time within your marital relationship. Be prepared to spring into action and use your first-aid kit.

CHAPTER 18 TIMELY TECHNIQUES

The Daily Decision to Love

While I fully believe that love is a strong and usable emotion, I must also accept the fact that *love is a decision*.

With the business and demands of daily life, it's easy to plop into bed fully exhausted at 11:00 P.M. and be off to work at 7:00 A.M. the next morning without ever giving a thought to your spouse occupying the other half of the bed!

The homemaking person can similarly be engaged with chores, chauffeuring kids, meetings, classes, committees, and various other duties.

As married couples, we must each make the decision daily to love our spouse if our marriage is to be kept in its proper perspective. This daily decision helps keep our relationship first.

To do this, we must focus on the goodness of our spouse and respond to it, not react. Don't react from where you are, but respond from where your spouse is.

When we recognize that love is a decision, we are reminded that a decision is an act of the will which involves choice and resolution. No one can make this decision for you; it is yours alone.

Marriage partners experiencing a rigorous disagreement may each feel that he or she is right, but in the process of insisting on his or her rightness, each partner is lonely and miserable. They need to mutually make the decision to love, so that they can be together in harmony.

Love is much like loyalty or "hanging in there." Even when on a particular day you don't feel particularly close, that love decision should be made. When you exchanged vows at the altar, the words "I will" were an affirmation that the matter was one involving a decision to which you agreed. This decision, if affirmed to each other daily—verbally or in your hearts—will greatly reduce the number of occasions requiring first aid in your marriage.

Accepting Your Spouse's Feelings

The decision to love involves our feelings. If our daily life reflects our decision to love, it will be characterized by our desire to share our deepest feelings with our lover, thus giving the relationship an openness and depth previously lacking.

None of us likes a relationship with no feelings, because the feeling of no feelings is commonly called the "blahs."

Characteristics of feelings:

1. Feelings form our foundation.
2. Feelings usually motivate our actions.
3. Feelings are never wrong.

    (The actions resulting from our feelings may be wrong, but no morality of rightness or wrongness should be attached to one's feelings.)
4. Feelings may feel bad or good.

5. Feelings are not a head trip but a heart trip.
6. Feelings get to the core of who I am.
7. Feelings in husband and wife are uniquely different.
8. Most people internalize feelings.
   (Many ailments are charged to the account of harboring feelings or keeping them pent up—for example, ulcers, high blood pressure.)
9. Understanding a person fully requires knowing his or her feelings.
10. Closeness and togetherness is greatly increased through sharing feelings.
11. Feelings are not thoughts or attitudes.
12. Although two people's thoughts may be the same, feelings are usually different.

Wouldn't you like to be able to discuss your innermost feelings with your spouse, knowing that he or she would not only tolerate but accept them and actually begin to feel them as you do?

The statements about feelings which you were actually too threatened to make could enrich your relationship, not produce problems.

"I feel threatened in new situations" is difficult for the masculine ego to admit, but this statement made to a wife can add trust and richness to a relationship.

"I feel like a piece of merchandise when you make love to me" when properly understood and accepted can accomplish much toward relationship improvement.

"I feel deeply hurt at this moment because of your actions" might achieve much more in the parent-child relationship than a good hard slap (although that's certainly needed at times).

The vehicle for sharing these feelings will be discussed in detail. There is a proper way.

When you share your feelings with your wife, it is like making a gift to her and letting her know you as you really are. You are letting her into your very heart, a place no one need go without your personal invitation.

Examining each other's feelings is not comparing *sameness* as much as exploring *differences*.

A husband should encourage his wife to share her feelings and describe them in detail. This he does by reaching out to her and she to him while maintaining openness about each other's feelings.

A mate should never reject his or her spouse's feelings, whether verbally or nonverbally, through facial expressions, a sigh, or other means. Remember, feelings are neither right nor wrong, so don't quarrel with them—just hand them over.

As a rule, if you can replace the word "feel" with the word "think" you're really talking about thoughts rather than feelings.

Example:

"I feel that you don't love me" is a statement in which you can insert "think" in the place of "feel." This usually indicates that your statement is really a thought rather than a feeling.

The statement "I feel warm all over and much love toward you" truly expresses a feeling, for placing "think" in the place of "feel" makes no sense.

When you share feelings, richness is added to the relationship. A "feeling life" shared with your mate can be every bit as exciting and rewarding as a shared sexual experience.

Sharing feelings is not a license to jump on your spouse by accusing him or her of being responsible for "all my feelings," nor is it a time to solve all marital problems and vent your spleen.

Physical health is aided by the ability of people to share inner frustrations, thereby reducing stress. Sharing feelings with your marriage partner not only adds richness but health and vitality to the relationship.

Love Notes

The practical way to share your feelings and act on your love is to turn your feelings into a love note.

By writing a note to each other daily you are in effect saying, "Here I am. I give myself fully exposed to you to have and to hold."

Expressing yourself on paper is also a commitment to your relationship. If writing were not important, you would see more oral contracts! When you write it, it's more apt to be acted on and evaluated by you.

The love note is a gift to each other and should be an honest expression of your feelings about a mutually-agreed-upon question.

Like any love note, it should begin with a loving greeting and end with a loving closing. It should be extremely personal, frequently mentioning your spouse by name. Take care to explain your feelings in fullest detail for your partner. Make it come alive. Be honest. Even feelings of anger can be tender. Share them.

Special care should be taken to avoid the trap of writing what you think your spouse wants to read. This practice lessens the integrity of the note and therefore its effectiveness.

In selecting the question to write about in the love note, it is important to focus on the present and not delve deeply into the past, reopening sores of an earlier vintage.

The note should be written seriously, not making light of each other's answers.

If you don't write in the same room, try to picture the one you love as you write.

As in an exercise or weight-reduction program, the greatest results are achieved through consistency. The same is true with the practice of the love note; consistency is the answer. Try to write one daily.

The most critical phase of the love note process is the presenting and receiving of it to each other.

When you've purchased a gift for a loved one, you don't throw it to him or her, but you present it with loving care.

A note is an even more valuable gift, since it contains your innermost feelings, which prior to this time you have felt unable to share.

Look at each other, hold hands, or embrace as you lovingly exchange your notes.

Read the notes together, following these simple rules:

1. Don't correct (spelling, wording).
2. Don't react or make comments.
3. Read twice.

    First time—read for the head to understand what has been written.

    Second time—read for the heart to understand the person who wrote the letter, while trying to experience the feelings which he or she has expressed.
4. Make certain the notes express feelings.
5. Write for no more than ten minutes.
6. Interact (we'll discuss this next).
7. Select the next day's question, then both partners write it down and exchange papers. The question written in your spouse's handwriting will assist you in keeping your mind on him or her as you write your love note.

Sample questions on which to base your love notes are listed below, although you should make up your own.

How do I feel when you're sick?
How do I feel when I see you after a long day?
How do I feel when I make a special sacrifice for you?
How do I feel when you decide to love me?
What qualities do I like best about you today? How does my answer make me feel?
What are my feelings when we go out socially?
What are my feelings about your daily work?
What are my feelings when we are separated?

Mutually decide upon a time each day when you can spend the ten minutes writing the love note.

Avoid writing the notes when you're dead tired at night. Your thoughts are either busied with all the activity of the day or you can hardly keep your eyes open. Surely it will be difficult under these circumstances to write a clear, concise, understandable love note to your spouse.

My wife and I make a practice of each taking the question of the day to our respective places of employment. We try to write for ten minutes during our lunch hour. As soon as we arrive home, prior to dinner, we complete our love notes, or, if we've both found time to complete them during the day, we exchange them and interact for ten minutes on our notes.

Pick a prime time when you're fresh. Let the kids know that this half-hour is yours.

You as a couple might be tempted to rebel at this point because someone has the audacity to ask you to daily write a ten-minute love note and then interact about its contents for another ten minutes.

"How can we ever find the time?"

If you don't deem your marriage important enough to

spend 1/72nd of your day solely concentrating on the man or woman you love, your priorities need examining.

Once you experience the resulting deepness of relationship through the love-note process, a day missed will be a rarity.

Interaction

After you lovingly exchange your notes, you should interact on the most important phase of one of the letters. You should mutually decide on what area seems most significant to both of you.

The notes will usually contain or deal with several separate feelings. If you try to interact on more than one, you may be beginning a telethon, whereas you should really limit your interaction to ten quality minutes.

If the interaction becomes too lengthy, outside pressures of children or other interruptions interfere and break concentration. Not limiting the interaction to ten minutes can also make the couple more hesitant to daily commit the required time.

When the ten minutes is over, we select our question for the next day, which is often based on the interaction which we weren't able to complete today.

The interaction always zeros in on feelings.

Begin the interaction by telling each other how you feel about each other's feelings expressed in the notes. Show that you're urgently interested. Hold hands or express love and understanding in some other nonverbal way.

After telling each other how you feel about each other's feelings, deal exclusively with the strongest feeling and interact exclusively on that area.

The member who did not write about the area of feelings you've decided to interact about begins to probe into the feelings of the writer by asking key questions which zero in on exactly how he or she feels in the situation described.

The partner not talking should make an intense effort to listen. *Really listen;* don't be preoccupied with thinking of your next question when he or she is speaking.

Questions continue to be asked by the spouse until he or she finally, through the answers, is told, "That's the feeling, that's exactly how I feel."

If you can reach that point, you truly have experienced the innermost feelings of your mate.

The acceptance and love which develop at that moment deepen and fulfill the relationship daily.

The kinds of questions asked of each other when you interact are:

1. Tell me more.
2. Is it like. . . ? and then describe how you think he or she wants you to feel, and how you imagine it is to feel the way your spouse is feeling.
3. How does your feeling make you feel physically?
4. What helps you to describe it more fully?
5. What other feelings are there?
6. How does it feel to feel the way you feel?
7. Have I ever described a feeling like yours to you? Tell me about how you remember that feeling of mine. How does it compare with your present feeling?
8. Have you ever felt this way before? How does it compare with those other times?
9. What have I said or done in past dialogues that helped you get out your feelings more?
10. What intensifies your feeling . . . lessens it?

11. How do you feel about revealing this feeling? Is there a difference in your reaction in the reflection and the dialogue?
12. Let your spouse know where you are in reaching out to his or her feelings.
13. Tell what helps you to respond better, to comprehend more.
14. Tell whether you are prejudiced toward him or her at this moment, and what helps you to become more prejudiced.
15. Tell whether you have any real desire to feel his or her feeling now, and what helps you to want your spouse's feeling.
16. Your spouse should tell you how he or she feels about your questions or your responses.

Use only one or two questions during any given interaction, to allow you to stay within the time constraints.

Phil and Karen wrote their love notes today in answer to the question, "How do I feel about today?"

The following statement was made by Phil to Karen in his daily love note. After reading the note, Phil and Karen chose this statement of feelings to interact on.

Statement of feeling:

"I really felt worthless and embarrassed today when the boss asked Charlie to prepare and present the report to the clients instead of me. And Charlie hasn't been working on it and isn't even a company officer."

Karen—"Tell me more, Phil."

Phil—"Well, I felt totally useless. I've worked on that project for three years and know it inside and out, and he picks Charlie."

Karen—"What other feelings are there, Phil?"

Phil—"I feel angry, I guess. I feel like punching old Johnson's lights out for picking Charlie."

Karen—"How does it feel to feel the way you feel?"

Phil—"Although I feel all the ways I mentioned, I feel guilty and ashamed for my feelings because I'm an adult and know life must go on. Charlie's had some bad breaks before, too, in his five years with the company."

Karen—"Phil, when Mr. Johnson picked Charlie for the presentation, did it feel like the time you didn't get the job with Suntex Corp.?"

Phil—"No, it felt much worse today. At least when I lost that job I knew the guy who got it had his Ph.D. in engineering, and I could accept that he got the job because of better training."

Karen—"Did you feel like the time before we were married when we were bowling with a large group and you asked me home but I had already accepted an invite?"

Phil—"Somewhat, but today was much deeper. I was better qualified than Charlie."

Karen—"Phil, once in eighth-grade physical education class, four captains were chosen to pick volleyball teams. The captains stood in front of us forty girls and slowly picked the girls, one by one. When twenty of us were left, I began to feel uncomfortable. When ten were unchosen and I was still among them, I felt terrible. I was much better than many of the girls already selected. As one-by-one the girls were picked, I began to feel more and more worthless and embarrassed. When the last captain picked me she said, loud enough for most of the girls to hear, 'Well, I guess I'm stuck with Karen.' Phil, is that how you felt today?"

Phil—"That's it, Karen. I think that's exactly how I felt today and still feel."

Karen was finally able to feel Phil's feeling, and Phil for

the first time felt that Karen felt what he felt. The closeness resulting from this daily dialogue on feelings will amaze you.

Pay specific attention to the fact that at no time did Karen judge Phil's feelings as "right" or "wrong." She just tried to feel them, and then not only tolerated them but accepted them.

Tolerating means "I put up with but don't get involved." Accepted means "I actually begin to feel within myself the feelings of another person."

The interaction you just read was based upon a feeling concerning an event which occurred during the day.

As you feel the value adding richness to your relationship, you will want to reach out to each other by interacting in many critical areas of life, such as:

1. Money
2. Health
3. Time
4. Work
5. Rest
6. Sexual relations
7. Marriage
8. Children
9. Relatives
10. Relationship to God
11. Atmosphere in the home
12. The big and little talents in our home
13. Latest mutual readings
14. Death
15. Life after death
16. Public affection

17. Supporting each other with children
18. Weight problems
19. Responsibility to aging parents
20. Activities outside the home
21. Future and retirement plans

Consistent daily interaction has many benefits, but among the greatest is the openness which the husband and wife feel as they realize they can share each and every feeling with each other and know it will be accepted.

This knowledge fosters trust, honesty, and deeper love.

People pay large fees for the privilege of lying on the couch of a psychiatrist to tell him their innermost feelings, knowing he will tolerate their feelings and not condemn them.

Doesn't it make more sense to share your feelings, free of charge, with someone who loves you, has stock in your life, and has learned to accept your feelings, not merely tolerate them?

Discarding Those Masks

Each one of us wears masks daily. We wear these because we need the approval of others around us, and our underlying insecurity warns us that unless we appear to be different from what we really are, we'll be rejected.

Some of us wear the masks of:

1. *Dedicated Hard Worker*

   He seeks the admiration of all as he exhibits total, uncompromising loyalty to tasks both at home and at work, apparently accepting his role willingly.

   With his mask discarded you may find a person who feels inferior and nonaccepted, and who begrudges every minute he plays that role. He wishes he could relax and be accepted as himself by his friends and family.

2. *Super Mother*

She seeks the admiration of all as she finishes her chores at midnight, rises early to prepare breakfast, keeps the kids looking like fashion plates, and her house could at any moment of the day be photographed to appear in *Home Beautiful*. She always puts her own desires aside to cater to everyone else's needs.

Peering under the mask, one sees a fearful little girl who feels that her acceptance and love is totally dependent on doing things. She feels she is on a merry-go-round which will never stop, and wonders "Is this all there is?"

3. *Macho Man*

As he finishes his weight-lifting, he enters the door announcing he's pressed ten pounds more tonight. He walks past the dirty dishes, not giving them a glance, even though his wife is hopelessly behind in her chores. He knows that men protect their family and provide for them but never do housework, show feelings, or cry.

Beneath this mask might well be revealed a person so intimidated that he feels the devotion to building brawn and muscle might be the answer to conquering his fears. He doesn't realize that a man secure about his manhood can partake in every home activity without being suspect.

4. *Good Humor Person*

"Isn't she just the cleverest person you've ever heard? She's witty and always the life of the party. Don't ever try to pull one over on her or she'll devastate you." Admiration is sought by demonstrating to all that she's never "down," but is always on top of everything.

Alone in her apartment, one finds a sad person often questioning her role and existence. She is fearful to some extent of answering a question truthfully for fear of nonacceptance, as she jokes about all, never answering more than surface deep.

Sometimes our masks are more than a cover-up, and reflect what we really want to be. In effect they're a goal.

As one receives favorable responses or compliments to the masks being worn, one can believe it is you, but deep down you know it really isn't.

Most people can accept compliments when they're merited, because the focus of the compliment is really us, but cannot accept compliments directed toward the mask we're perpetuating.

At times we are under the mistaken impression that we really need to wear masks. Some people wear masks their entire lives because of basic, underlying insecurity, but such mask-wearing constitutes living a lie and false advertising.

Only when we feel secure in ourselves and others' acceptance of us and our feelings do we dare peel down to the real us.

In marriage, discarding masks is imperative. Through love notes and interaction techniques this can be accomplished, allowing enrichment to result.

Touching and Showing

During the last several years, much has been written and said concerning nonverbal communication.

Body language is a frequent topic discussed on many talk shows and in popular newspapers. A person who is well-trained can supposedly perceive what message you're sending him by the way you're sitting, the position of your legs, whether you're leaning forward into his "space" or leaning back, the directness of your eye contact, and the pursing of your lips. Whether in reality anyone can be astute enough to accurately interpret all our inner feelings by our body positions is highly questionable, but without question, nonverbal messages can be given loud and clear.

If you're like me, one disapproving glance from my wife from across the room can stop my story dead in its tracks.

Two fingers held high in the air by a coach will cause eleven football players to change their defensive alignment.

One finger pointed heavenward may create a deep feeling of camaraderie between believers in Jesus Christ, while another finger raised on that same hand may result in a week's suspension from school.

A loving look from a partner connotes "yes."

A raised hand from a third-grader means "call on me."

Her hand reaching out to mine, "I need you and love you," gives the receiver a warm, loved feeling.

A shared tear means "I'm happy, "I'm sad," or "I feel the hurt like you."

At times, nonverbal communication says so much more than mere words. As you throw your arms around a grieving loved one who has just suffered great loss, that embrace says so much more than one's feeble attempts to verbally console.

Feelings can only be partially shared through words, but when supplemented by nonverbal communication, those words assume deeper meaning and intensity.

Touching is an important aspect of life from birth through death.

How many little girls do you know who don't have stuffed animals in their bedrooms? Many sleep with them because this touching provides company, caring, and security. Although an inanimate object to you and me, Snoopy is a "toucher," and is real to that five-year-old. He touches back and says "I care" by never getting up and walking away, while giving excuses of all the work he must do.

Many elderly widows have cats in their homes. Widows touch cats, and in their way cats touch back. When you pet a cat it never runs away, but just sidles up a little closer and strokes back, thereby saying, "I care." It doesn't approve or disapprove of you; it just stays.

All our lives we want to be touched, and yet when we get married and have the greatest opportunity afforded, many people omit that important aspect of their behavior, thus shortchanging themselves and their mates.

The hug when you come home, the held hands when you ask the blessing at dinner, the arm around the waist as you take that walk, the gentle massage of her neck while she watches TV—all convey an important message and offer enrichment to your relationship.

Mistakenly, many husbands feel that touching must lead to sex. How wrong this belief is. When each touch results in an attempt at sexual intercourse, a wife may justifiably believe that every touch by the husband has an ulterior motive and must lead to his sexual gratification whether she feels like reciprocating or not.

Some of the most meaningful and satisfying experiences in marriage can be shared by lying in an embrace as you both doze off, or tenderly holding hands in front of a warm winter fire.

Touching and holding someone you love should produce gratification in both partners, for it says very loudly, "I care and you are important to me."

Some people omit touching as they explain, "I'm just not a toucher. It doesn't feel natural to me."

The first time you drove a car it didn't seem natural either, yet you didn't exclude that skill from your life, but repeated it over and over until it became a natural and important part of your life.

Touch to say "I love you" and nurture that habit. It will add much depth to your relationship and become an integral part of your life as it speaks louder than your words.

How to Fight

"No matter how well we are communicating with our marriage partners, there are bound to be some areas of disagreement. I have heard some couples claim they have never had a difference of opinion during all of their married life. What a drab and colorless existence they must have had; the couple either possessed very little personal individuality or else were afraid to express their true inner feelings. It is hard to believe that God ever made two people so alike in every way that their opinions coincided in everything."*

All couples will experience brief spats from time to time. When they do, how the partners fight may determine whether the relationship suffers or grows.

If you never fight, I'm concerned about the health of your relationship.

Ground rules are necessary for healthy fighting:

1. Don't hit below the belt.

When one or both partners attack personalities and

---

*From page 89 of *Marriage Is for Love*, by Richard L. Strauss, © 1973 by Tyndale House Publishers, Wheaton, Illinois. Used by permission.

not the problem, the fight can seldom be constructive. Never degrade, demean, or call names. Swearing and vulgarity directed personally cause deep wounds.

2. Don't wear your belt around your neck.

   It's as unfair to do this as it is to "hit below the belt." Oversensitivity to the point of declaring any discussion off-limits will prevent constructive growth.

3. Be honest and speak the truth in love.

   Dishonesty breaks trust. Many problems could be remedied if partners were honest. If you are dishonest with your mate, you're actually excluding him or her from your life.

   Honesty can hurt, so present your facts and honest feelings in love, with utmost consideration for your mate.

4. Refrain from using generalities and gross exaggerations.

   These belittle and ignite anger. "You never show concern," "You're always ungrateful." Very few of these statements are true, and the chasm created when they're stated greatly reduces the chance of positive outcomes.

5. Always finish your fights.

   If you walk out without a conclusion, the unsettled abrasions will begin to fester and the mind will tend to amplify the seriousness of the disagreement. Talk it out, even if it doesn't quite end in a neatly tied package with "resolutions forevermore."

   "Hit-and-run" arguments usually create in the mate a feeling that he or she doesn't merit the time or effort required to talk a problem through.

6. Try to touch while you're fighting.

   If you have ever tried this, you'll quickly observe that the fighting can still entail honesty and disagreement, but somehow any desire to win is overshadowed by a caring and fair attitude.

7. Listen—truly listen.

   Most often when you're fighting, as your partner talks you're really not concentrating on what he or she is saying, but your mind is actively framing your next question, ready to pounce in and defend your position.

   Next time, totally concentrate on his or her statements.

   At times it is especially difficult for men to listen. They are culturized as "doers" rather than "receivers" and "providers" rather than "consumers."

   The wise married man soon realizes that he must listen and receive if he is to be able to continue giving to his spouse.

8. "Don't let the sun go down on your anger."

   These divinely inspired words are packed with wisdom. Going to sleep with anger in your heart is destructive to the marriage relationship. I'm not suggesting that you become dishonest by claiming that everything is okay when it's not, nor am I suggesting that you condescend by saying, "Well, okay, you're right, dear" so that you can attain pseudo-compliance with the Scripture quoted above. In this case, both your spouse and God know you're lying.

   I'm suggesting that an honest way to comply is to

state to your spouse, "I know we aren't together in our feelings about this situation, and we can discuss them again tomorrow when I get home. I do want you to know, however, that I love you and that's why it's important that we work through these times. Good night, dear." Try it. God doesn't give instructions without providing a reward for following them.

Accepting Self and Spouse

A poster proudly hangs in the "marriage encounter" seminar room which states, "God doesn't make junk."

Most people realize that perfection is not one of their attributes. Shortcomings and failures are part of our everyday lives, and through them we are reminded of our fallibility.

God reminds us of this when He states, "All have sinned and come short of the glory of God."

But dwelling on our condition and perpetuating a feeling of worthlessness is certainly not what God intends. This attitude, if nurtured, is detrimental to our personal well-being and deadly to our marriage relationship.

Unfairly, most of us view a virtue as a virtue only if it is *always* present, even though a weakness is considered a weakness if it is *ever* present!

God looked upon His creation, of which I am a part, and said, "It is good." Christ accepts me and thinks so highly of my potential that He gave His very Son to bring me into fellowship with Him.

I don't have to *come across* as something; I *am* something. God doesn't make mistakes.

If we cannot accept and love ourselves, we will not be able to accept and love others.

The success I have in accepting and living with myself will, to a large degree, determine my ability to accept and live with others.

If I make the decision not to accept myself, it keeps me from fullness and prevents me from totally accepting my spouse.

A man overcome by inferiority and feelings of worthlessness can produce severe problems in marriage, as he will require constant reassurance from his wife to allow him to somewhat accept himself. His efforts will be totally focused on his needs, not considering the needs of his wife. In order to satisfy him, her near-total energies must be devoted to reinforcing his. This relationship is destined to failure.

Just as dangerous in the marriage relationship is the super-egoist who considers himself always right and above reproach. When you're on top, you can only look down, and this doesn't foster a positive relationship.

We must accept ourselves as God has made us, neither dwelling on what we consider to be our inferiorities nor haughty about our suspected strengths. Only then can we accept others, including our spouse, as they are. This is a prerequisite to the establishment of fullness in our marriage relationship.

Accepting Shortcomings

When we repeat our marriage vows we make every effort to avoid stumbling over the words, yet the impact of some phrases like "For better or for worse" doesn't attain real significance until after the honeymoon.

Each week seems to reveal another new facet of our mate, and some of these facets we love, while others we deplore.

Occasionally we evaluate ourselves, and if we do so truthfully we become aware of our shortcomings. It's amazing how tolerant we can be of our *own* shortcomings, even to the point of rationalizing them away!

Yet our mate may possess shortcomings of equal or lesser degree, and they are viewed by us as much more severe.

Guidelines for accepting shortcomings of your mate:

1. Review what you consider to be a shortcoming.
2. Answer honestly the question, "By whose standard is that characteristic a shortcoming?"
3. Objectively observe other people; does that shortcoming also appear to be evident in them?
4. Read current works on the characteristics of the marriage relationship to see if the apparent shortcoming is rare or common. You may find that you're judging too harshly and from the wrong perspective.
5. Review the strengths and positive characteristics of your mate that attracted you to him or her in the first place.
6. If, after taking these actions, the shortcoming is still a source of concern and still evokes an emotional response on your part, talk with your spouse about it.
7. When talking, be honest but speak in love, realizing that certainly you also have some deficiencies that are a concern to him or her.
8. Interact about the characteristic or deficiency which bothers you. Tell him or her in a way that leaves no doubt that you love him or her, that it's the shortcoming alone that is the source of your concern.

9. Assure him or her that your continued love does not depend on abolishing this shortcoming, but that you knew you could share your concern with acceptance.
10. Indicate to your mate that he or she should also feel free to express openly those concerns about you which bother him or her.
11. Be prepared to make as much effort becoming more tolerant as your mate makes in eliminating the source of concern.
12. Realize that a mature person adjusts to the things he or she cannot change.

By following these guidelines the deficiency could be declared invalid, it could be partially or totally corrected, the mate bothered by it could become more tolerant, or no change could occur.

I can guarantee, however, that merely discussing the concern in love will enrich your relationship.

Learning to Forgive and Apologize

The ability to forgive is sadly lacking in many relationships.

As a mate you may have been wronged unjustly. When your spouse seeks your forgiveness, or even if he or she doesn't, love demands that you forgive his or her actions.

If forgiveness is withheld, the relationship cannot be restored to its original harmony.

The longer we withhold forgiveness, the more difficult the act of forgiveness becomes as the disagreement assumes inordinate proportions.

When we genuinely forgive, our negative feelings toward our mate pass, and then and only then can our love flow as freely as previously.

As the warmth of forgiveness surrounds your mate, the dividends begin to drift your way as he or she reciprocates in a positive way.

Apologizing is integrally related to forgiveness, and forgiveness usually follows on the heels of the apology. Unfortunately, it is difficult for most people to apologize, and some even consider the act a sign of weakness.

With some people it is more important to determine who's right and who's wrong than it is to restore the relationship to complete fellowship.

Apologizing should be—

1. specific. Tell exactly what you're apologizing for; saying "I'm sorry for everything" (the blank-check approach) reeks of insincerity.
2. complete. Don't apologize and end with "But if you hadn't ———." A sincere apology omits focusing attention on others; it simply concentrates on you.
3. sincere. No humor is fitting; let the spouse know that your apology comes from the heart. If you don't feel you can be sincere, your apology may do more harm than good.
4. viewed as a sign of strength. Strength is evident when one can accomplish a difficult task, and certainly admitting that you're wrong is just that. Many people (especially men) believe that admitting they're wrong is a sign of weakness. But by owning up to your weaknesses and being honest, the respect which your spouse and others involved have for you will be increased.
5. a vehicle for restoring fellowship. The greatest Teacher of all time taught that until you were reconciled in your relationship to others you could never experience true fellowship. When you

apologize you are relieved, and immediately (or shortly thereafter) you can feel the spirit of fellowship being restored.
6. accepted in love. We owe acceptance of the sincere apology to ourself, our mate, and the relationship.

Failure to accept the apology, or to accept the apology with an "I-told-you-so" attitude, is devastating to your mate and will increase the difficulty experienced by the spouse in future attempts at apology.

Scheduling Time Together

Most relationships could be vastly improved if time was set aside daily for being together. I believe that improvement would be noted even if the daily interlude consisted of total silence, for love can be felt.

If even *silence* can be felt, twenty minutes per day devoted to *communication* between husband and wife—utilizing the techniques discussed—could revolutionize your marriage.

Unfortunately, most married couples live the lives of "married singles."

The wife's responsibilities are:

children
transportation
art class
the inside of the home
bridge
cooking
etc.

The husband's responsibilities are:

his job
the outside of the home
family finances
repair
garbage
etc.

We begin to let this division of responsibilities lead us into separate lives.

During your courtship years you couldn't spend enough time together. Even if your girl was a hundred miles away, you still found time to go to school, work two jobs, and see her three times a week. Nothing could keep you two apart. You discussed every little thing from your clothes to your kid sister to world problems and your cooperative solution.

But times have changed, and now you know you can't possibly waste all that time both working on the same area of concern. You must stay departmentalized for maximum efficiency.

As you accept more and more responsibilities and incur more obligations, both lists grow, until soon every minute of every day is budgeted separately.

The only time spent together is when you fall into bed, and time spent sleeping is not really considered quality communication time. Fellowship doesn't take place by osmosis!

Soon the only communication you have is communication about things and events. There's no time for personal concerns, since these subjects require too much discussion time.

Other factors contribute to our noncommunication.

Television has done much to consume our time, to the detriment of family communication.

Did you ever attempt to talk in a room where TV was being watched? As you speak, others look askance or hush you so that every word of the program can be heard. "No communication allowed."

Many families have solved that noise factor by buying two or three TV's, or one for every person, so that total concentration can be devoted to the almighty tube, with hardly a word spoken. We don't even have to hush anymore!

Dinah Shore recently spoke about an L.O.P. syndrome.

Even when there's nothing worth watching on TV, we keep it turned on by switching channels to the Least Objectionable Program!

What a sad commentary on our society! Watching a test pattern is better than communicating with the person or people we love!

Many married couples have in reality become "ships passing in the night." They know of each other's existence, but they avoid each other and aren't really involved with each other.

The situation between parent and child is no different.

A commitment of twenty minutes per day to a relationship could literally make a world of difference in its quality.

What a lesson we could learn from Jesus Christ!

As we read the Scriptures, we find that Jesus had a constant demand for His time due to His charisma, power, and position.

The pressure on our time is insignificant compared to His; everyone needed Him.

Time and time again Jesus allotted time and interrupted His activities to speak to the person in need.

He didn't speak abruptly or reply curtly, but in many cases would actually take the time to relate an entire parable to add clarity to the conversation.

Could we learn from the Master? No wonder He continually drew people to Him and had such a tremendous impact on all of history!

Our marriage relationship should be a most important area in our lives. If it is in disarray, every facet of our life is colored negatively.

Can we commit 1/72nd of our day to enrich it? I think so.

Time together is a must. To arrange this I may have to reevaluate my activities and begin eliminating some of *mine* and she some of *hers* in order to provide for some of *ours*.

Setting Goals for Marriage

When something is important to us, we rarely leave it to chance.

If you are directing the church choir and that activity is important to you, you set goals to lead that group toward its performance potential. You wouldn't leave the group's development to chance. Regular practices, dress rehearsals, coordination with pianists, and in-service training might well be part of your overall plan to insure success.

Yet many people get married and believe that their great mutual love will keep the marriage beautiful, with never a thought to establishing goals for their marriage.

1. *Awareness level*

    At this level a couple knows what their goal is, but no action is taken.

    Example: We want our marriage to result in effective communication.

2. *Internalization level*

At this level each person involved in the goal personalizes his or her desire to achieve the goal.

Example: I feel I really want to communicate effectively with my mate.

3. *Action level*

At this level action takes place toward making the goal a reality.

Example: The couple reserves the first half-hour when husband comes home to communicate.

Unfortunately, most couples don't set any goals for their marriage. While some couples do set goals, they may reach only the first two levels of goals and never reach the *action* level necessary to make their marriage effective.

Planned action is necessary to guide a marriage to fullness.

With your spouse, arrive at mutually-agreed-upon goals for your marriage, then devise a plan of action which allows for progress toward goal attainment.

Put the plan to work.

Remember, inactivity signifies a lack of commitment to your marriage relationship.

Extending Love to Others

There are two bodies of water that are fed by the Jordan River. One is called the Sea of Galilee, and it is teeming with fish and is frequently marked by many people in the hustle and bustle of activity. This is where Jesus walked, performed many miracles, and spoke to the multitudes. The other sea is the Dead Sea. There is no life in it whatever, and it is an isolated body of water with little or no activity.

It is interesting to note that both of these bodies of water are fed by the same river—the Jordan—and yet one is teeming and alive while the other is vacant and dead. What is the difference? The Jordan River flows into the Sea of Galilee, and because of its altitude the water can also flow out. The Jordan also flows into the Dead Sea, but because of its exceptionally low altitude the water cannot flow out. Therefore the water becomes stagnant and cannot support life.

This is a great picture of our love. Much love can be flowing in, but unless we also pass that love on to other people, we are faced with tremendous stagnation. But if we pass the love on to other people we become alive, exuberant, and vital.

So it is with our marriage.

If we allow our mutual love to flow freely to our children, our friends, and others, our marriage will be exuberant and alive.

If we fail to share our mutual love, our marriage may become stagnant and characterized by lack of vitality.

Once you begin sharing mutual love, and you become aware of how much enrichment enters your life, you won't want it any other way.

Love is truly love when you give it away.

CHAPTER 19
IF FIRST-AID FAILS

The first-aider does everything within his power to care for the victim of an accident or sudden illness. Many times his actions are sufficient, and no doctor need be consulted or called to check the victim.

In many serious cases, however, the prompt care of a doctor is required to prevent more serious injury or death.

You and your mate can solve many problems in your marriage relationship through correct application of the suggested techniques in this book.

However, if you conscientiously apply the suggested techniques over a reasonable period of time and still notice no improvement in your relationship, professional counseling should be considered.

As a parallel example, the many-faceted business you operate has run into problems. Although you signed what you believed was a five-year lease with an option to buy, you recently have been advised that you now face possible eviction due to a technicality overlooked in the lease agreement.

A relocation of the thriving business at this time would certainly cause a reversal and might even force a foreclosure.

You decide to seek legal counsel, so you as the owner of the business investigate the firm of Katz & Joseph.

Mr. Katz assures you that his firm represents quality, and cites an excellent reputation in criminal law and large client settlements in divorce cases and liability actions.

When you ask him about their real estate lawyer, Katz openly states that they haven't handled any real estate law questions, but assures you that they will research the case well and will provide good service.

You politely excuse yourself and begin the law firm search anew, since a decision involving your entire business future cannot be left in the hands of a law firm which has never experienced and successfully handled problems in your area of critical need.

We can readily sympathize with you as this business owner. Most of us will agree that your decision was wise, for certainly anything affecting our future security and happiness demands the best and most effective resources we can get.

We take great pains to see that our business and financial problems are cared for by obtaining the best resource persons available, yet time and again we fail to seek help with our marital problems, and when we finally do seek help we select people who are as ill-prepared to treat our problems as Katz was to handle the problem involving real estate law.

As Christians, each of us has three areas of life which should affect every decision we make, every task we perform, and every relationship we take part in. These areas are the physical, the mental, and the spiritual.

People who don't have a personal relationship with Christ cannot really understand or deal with the spiritual area of our human existence.

A marriage counselor can be highly trained in all areas

of counseling techniques, and even be highly recommended, yet be no more effective for us than Katz was for his potential client.

Mathematically speaking, the secular counselor in question can treat only two-thirds of our total being, since he is unqualified in the spiritual area which we possess. He is prepared to treat only the physical and mental areas of our existence.

I once had a friend who before his conversion experience stated, "I can read the Bible over and over and not understand a word of it." Since becoming a member of the family of God, he is amazed that when he reads the same passage over and over, the Holy Spirit provides a different lesson and deeper meaning with each experience.

A person who hasn't experienced a spiritual rebirth cannot understand a spiritual book, or a spiritual person, or a spiritual couple.

A person who has never experienced the love of Christ personally cannot comprehend His importance in the marriage relationship. Such a person has never experienced:

1. the openness to God which we feel as we become open with our mate.
2. the growing openness to God and spouse in a marriage based on God's love.
3. the relief and joy we receive when we realize that God accepts us and our relationship even though God is fully aware of all our inner feelings.
4. the bond of love shared with other couples who possess Christ's love.
5. the joy of knowing that Christ is interested in the quality of our marital relationship.

6. the clarity of lessons taught about marriage in the Scriptures.
7. the depth and warmth which can be added to a relationship as mates pray together in love.
8. the beauty which Christ can add to all activities which the marriage partners experience together.

If you and your spouse are seeking counseling assistance in your marriage, ask the prospective counselor whether he deals with the spiritual aspect of the marriage relationship.

If the answer is no, or if the importance of the spiritual is downgraded, seek another counselor.

I am not suggesting that a secular marriage counselor cannot assist a Christian couple achieve an improved relationship, for certainly he can familiarize the couple with the latest proven techniques designed to improve communication, accept each other's feelings, recognize danger areas, and correct attitudinal problems.

But I do state emphatically that only counselors who have experienced the reality of God can lead God's couples to marital fullness.

One established fact is certain: no counselor can effectively contribute to improving the relationship of any couple seeking help if that couple is not honest.

They must be honest with themselves, with the counselor, and with God.

They must also recognize the fact that little or no progress will be made toward solving their problem unless they are willing to acknowledge the problem as their own.

Constructive change and improvement always involves some discomfort and risk.

CHAPTER 20
FIRST-AID PRIORITIES

As the helicopter landed on the road in Wrightwood, California, two Highway Patrolmen raced in opposite directions to block the flow of traffic.

The doctor, paramedics, and members of the ski patrol swiftly placed the stretchers containing the splinted bodies in the helicopter for transportation to the nearest hospital.

The faces of the victims revealed the anguish of severe pain produced by the accident and associated injuries.

The scene was almost ironic. The victims were rendered helpless and therefore unable to assist themselves. The paramedics, although trained, were unable to assist beyond a certain point. Even the doctor, with all his years of excellent training, was unable to piece the victims together and send them on their way.

I'm sure the victims were admitted to the Victorville Hospital and were given the best medical care available, yet with all this attention, first aid, professional handling, and medical care, healing was not assured.

My mind flashed back to the summer of 1975, when my mother was diagnosed as having cancer which was likely to be terminal.

As they rolled her out of the surgical recovery room toward the elevator, my dad and I approached the surgeon. Upon questioning, he indicated, "The surgery went beautifully, but now it's up to God. I can do so much, but only God can heal."

The first-aid priority for physical ailments is:

1. The victim assists himself if he is able to do so.
2. The first-aider assists the victim and calls the doctor if the injury is severe.
3. The doctor treats the patient and hospitalizes him if necessary.
4. The hospital administers required treatment.
5. Specialists are brought in if it is necessary.
6. After men have done all within their power, God heals.

Note the similarities between the first-aid priorities for the treatment of physical injury and the following priorities for the treatment of injury within the marriage relationship:

1. Marriage partners assist themselves with self-counseling if able.

A definite sequence of approach exists in first-aid treatment for an ailing marriage relationship. When the relationship is suffering, the most logical persons to administer first aid to the relationship are the marriage partners.

As Marcia Lasswell and Norman Lobsenz state in their book *No-Fault Marriage,* "Certainly no struggle is more common than marriage, and no comrade closer than a wife or husband. Thus, for a couple to work together on their relationship, to be their own therapists, seems both logical and fitting. It is also likely to be highly effective once the necessary skills are mastered."*

In helping themselves, some couples choose to share their concerns and problems with trusted friends. Many counselors frown on this practice, since the sharing of intimate problems may cause additional problems. Confidences can be broken and the relationship can be affected once intimate details are shared out of the marriage.

Many couples find resource books on marriage an effective tool providing self-counseling for their own marriage. Excellent books by qualified psychologists, such as Dr. James Dobson, can be used to add insight and understanding to one's source of problems.

2. Seek professional help if necessary.

If the couples experiencing marital problems use intelligently and regularly the self-counseling techniques taught in this book and fully detailed in Chapter 18, there should be decided improvement in the marriage relationship.

If the couple notes no improvement after several months of consistent applications of the newly acquired techniques, they should seek out a qualified marriage counselor.

The counselor's task is to assist the partners in dealing with their own problems so they will be able to handle subsequent problems by themselves.

At times it is necessary to employ a professional counselor to assure an unbiased mutual party who can approach the problems without being involved emotionally.

---

*Excerpt from *No-Fault Marriage*, by Marcia Lasswell and Norman M. Lobseng. Copyright © 1976 by Marcia Lasswell and Norman M. Lobseng. For use by permission of Doubleday & Company, Inc.

Often his experience will allow and encourage the partners to approach their problem from a new and refreshing perspective which provides additional impact.

3. *God is the Great Healer.*

Even as God alone heals the physical, He alone is responsible for a complete healing of the suffering or injured marriage relationship and its progression back to total fullness.

Certainly, self-counseling and professional counseling contribute much to the healing process, but the introduction of Jesus Christ into a relationship adds a new dimension and depth which cannot be achieved in any other way.

Christ's love indwelling each marriage partner allows them to make the marriage a sacred three-way relationship between the partners and an infinite, all-knowing, all-powerful, compassionate, and loving Lord.

God's plan for marriage is not to have the couple so self-sufficient and self-reliant that they don't need Him.

Many couples have come to think of God as the Marines: "They're always there when you need them." But God desires our daily reliance on Him and our daily fellowship with Him.

God wants only the best for our lives as couples. Anything which heals, integrates, or puts together is of God.

Marriage should be a total commitment of two total persons for their total life made possible through a total Lord.

CHAPTER 21
PRESCRIPTION OF THE GREAT PHYSICIAN

"If they had more faith they wouldn't be having marital problems."

"If they were only more committed to God, their marriage problems would be solved."

"They must not be praying about their marital problems, or improvement would be evident."

My blood almost curdles when I hear such statements attributing the total blame for marital discord to shortcomings in the area of faith, commitment, and prayer life.

I'm tempted to ask the person assessing the troubled couples' spiritual maturity, "Aren't we also to blame for their marital discord, since we as members of the same body of Christ should be upholding them in prayer? Maybe if our faith, our commitment, and our prayer life were stronger and more vital their marital problems would be solved."

Faith, commitment, and prayer are vitally important to relationship improvement, for God often rewards a closer walk with Himself by providing keener insights, increased understanding, increased wisdom, and other abilities which if applied could facilitate marital improvement. But unless these are accompanied by a corresponding commitment to evaluate one's own marriage, to acknowledge the existing problems, to employ proven techniques for marriage improvement, to seek professional counseling when necessary—in short, to exert a maximum effort to make the marriage successful—faith, commitment, and prayer can be used as a cop-out.

Faith, commitment, and prayer are vital elements in our personal relationship with Jesus Christ and are therefore interwoven into our Christian marital experience.

A victim of marital discord, however, can possess intense faith that his marital disharmony will be remedied but see absolutely no positive results unless he or she focuses on the problems at hand, and with his or her mate makes a concerted effort to heal the relationship.

Likewise, a couple may possess an unwavering commitment to each other, to their marriage, and to Christ, yet watch their relationship slowly deteriorate due to their stubbornness or unwillingness to devote a concerted effort toward its improvement.

Prayer is a resource available to every believer, and its power cannot be denied. Yet prayer alone, without a concurrent effort aimed at improving the relationship, often proves to no avail as the marital discord continues unchecked.

Occasionally one of my daughters, when leaving for school in the morning, hollers out, "Dad, remember to pray for me as I take my algebra test." My response is always, "Before I can pray for you, how much time did you spend studying for the exam?" If her answer is "none," I let her know that prayer will not help, because God does not honor a lack of effort on our part by magically supplying information we have not studied. In effect, God does not do our work for us, but often honors our efforts with success.

Unfortunately, many believers feel that it is God's responsibility to keep their marriage sound. This is not the case, for if it were, God would not have offered so many specific suggestions for maintaining and building an enriched marriage.

As believers we are often guilty of offering trite phrases or using religious jargon with couples or individuals in need of help. Sometimes we do this to relieve our own guilt, so that we can feel we have met our Christian responsibility. At other times we offer these acceptable religious phrases because we lack the knowledge to say something helpful or appropriate for the current situation. We believe that some catch-all phrase will always be acceptable: "Everything will work out"; "God loves you two"; "Time heals all wounds"; "She'll be back."

When we are experiencing marital problems, are we really naive enough to feel that we can suddenly lay claim to increased faith, increased commitment, or a more conscientious prayer life, and that the Lord will immediately undo all the hurts and inconsiderate acts occurring over many years of marriage, and will heal our relationship without a corresponding effort on our part?

I strongly believe that the Lord expects us to exert a maximum effort in order to achieve maximum results, and a quality marriage is a maximum result.

I frequently have occasion to think about a friend of mine who traveled around the Midwest as an evangelist. He related the story of a large, strong, rawboned country preacher who searched for gatherings of people as he passed from town to town. He would often speak to groups of men gathered in front of the general store, or to groups of people as they picnicked in the park on Sundays. On one occasion, as he was speaking to a large crowd in the park of a Midwest community, he was heckled by another man who mounted a tree stump and started proclaiming in a loud voice, "If you're real, God, knock me off this tree stump." The preacher continued but was interrupted repeatedly by the same statement, "If you're real, God, knock me off this tree stump." The preacher walked slowly and methodically out from behind his makeshift pulpit, sauntered over to the stump, reached his arm way back, and knocked the heckler completely off the stump and onto his back.

The crowd watched in amazement as the preacher looked down at the heckler and said in a loud and firm voice, "I never ask the Lord to do anything I can handle myself." Although some criticized the preacher for handling the problem in that way, I think we must adapt more of this type of attitude in our marital relationship. I am not proposing that one abandon his faith, his commitment, and his prayer life. Far from it. If anything, that commitment should be increased. However, we must realize that the Lord blesses a maximum effort on our part to handle the everyday problems and trials of life, including those found in maintaining a marital relationship.

We wouldn't expect to stay home from work for a lengthy duration without receiving a loss of salary with its possible effect on our family's standard of living; yet we often exert no effort at all to produce a quality marriage for long periods of time but still expect our marriage to continue effectively or even to grow in richness and maturity. Such will not be the case.

Faith, commitment, and prayer must be accompanied by our efforts to improve our relationship and to solve our marriage problems.

James 2:17, 18, states, " 'So you see, it isn't enough just to have faith. You must also do good to prove that you have it. Faith that doesn't show itself by good works is no faith at all—it is dead and useless.' But someone may well argue,

'You say the way to God is by faith alone, plus nothing; well, I say that good works are important too, for without good works you can't prove whether you have faith or not; but anyone can see that I have faith by the way I act.'"

Although this portion of Scripture refers to true faith evidenced by works, I cannot help but feel that it also has direct application to the marriage relationship.

Faith that your disharmonious relationship will abruptly become melodious may very well be "dead and useless" unless your faith is accompanied by a committed effort to resolve the problems. James 2:20 states, "Fool! When will you ever learn that 'believing' is useless without *doing* what God wants you to? Faith that does not result in good deeds is not real faith."

Even believing, or commitment, without a concerted effort will not produce harmonious marriage.

Don't use Christ or the elements of faith, commitment, and prayer as cop-outs. Christ stands with open arms ready to embrace and eagerly assist all victims of deteriorating and unfulfilled relationships, but He expects to see a commensurate effort on the part of the marriage partners.

The Great Physician desires nothing less than for you and your spouse to experience ultimate joy and blessing in your marital relationship. As Christian couples, we all have the potential to experience bountiful marriage.

When we "sinned and fell short of the glory of God," God was so grieved that His compassion compelled Him to send His son to die in our place and reconcile us to Himself. Jesus paid our penalty and took upon Himself the sin of the world so we could have eternal life and fellowship with Him.

Whenever we fall short of the potential given us by Christ in any area of our life, Christ is grieved and provides a plan for us to heal the shortcoming, so that through His loving prescription we can achieve our maximum potential in that area of life.

The Word of God provides a pattern for marriage which greatly enhances marital success and richness.

Let us look at what the Great Physician has prescribed for successful marriage.

As with all prescriptions, the desired results will not be obtained unless action is taken to follow the prescription, and action in the marriage relationship requires committed effort.

Prescription

1. Recognize that God has ordained the divine institution of marriage and therefore has a stake in your marital success. Genesis 2:24 states, "For this cause a man shall leave his father and his mother, and shall cleave to his wife, and they shall become one flesh" (NASB).

Since God has ordained the institution, it logically follows that you should involve Him in your marriage for optimum enrichment.

This involvement occurs through the study of Scriptures, and through prayer requesting His blessing on your relationship.

2. Recognize that God created your spouse to be a companion who equally benefits with you by making your marriage a success. Genesis 2:18 states, "And the Lord God said, It is not good that the man should be alone; I will make him an helpmeet for him" (KJV).

To be effective, a helpmate assumes a position of neither superiority or inferiority, but a partner working side-by-side with input into every situation.

3. Your marriage should be guided by the fact that your primary responsibility in marriage is to love and care for *your mate first,* your children second, your relations third, fellow Christians fourth, and others fifth. Ephesians 5:31 states, "For this cause a man shall leave his father and mother, and shall cleave to his wife, and the two shall become one flesh" (NASB). It is important to realize that if a marriage is to be successful, these priorities must be maintained. The Scriptures are careful to point out that our love and commitment to our spouse ranks significantly above our love and commitment to even our parents. Unless we recognize this fact, even children and in-law problems may interfere with the maintenance of God's priorities and our relationship.

4. Enjoy sex. God meant for sex to be enjoyed to its fullest and that the sex experience would contribute to the overall richness of the marital relationship. Hebrews 13:4 states, "Marriage is honorable in all, and the bed undefiled" (KJV). In his book *Thoroughly Married,* Dennis Guernsey states, "There is something alive about couples who have a creative love life. By creative, I mean they are free to do and enjoy what feels good to them. Whether it's oral-genital sex or some new and revolutionary position, what makes it right is that it feels good to them. Sexual practices change from culture to culture and it is this influence that makes one practice right or wrong. Again, the rule of thumb would be to never do anything that would offend the other. But if both agree, then, in my opinion, you're free."*

Many a man or woman has gotten involved with a

---

*From *Thoroughly Married,* by Dennis Guernsey, © 1975. Used by permission of Word Books, Publisher, Waco, Texas.

member of the opposite sex outside marriage because his or her mate has been insensitive to their psychological and sexual needs.

5. Submit as described in the Scriptures. The subject of submission in marriage seems to be controversial even among Christians.

I have rarely been part of a discussion involving submission where some resentment did not surface. Ephesians 5:22-24 states, "Wives, be subject to your own husbands, as to the Lord. For the husband is the head of the wife, as Christ also is the head of the church, He Himself being the Savior of the body. But as the church is subject to Christ, so also the wives ought to be to their husbands in everything" (NASB).

In his book *Marriage Is For Love*, Richard L. Strauss states:

> One of the most hotly debated and fiercely denounced concepts in all the Bible is that "the husband is the head of the wife, even as Christ is the head of the Church." This is the Biblical doctrine of headship. Properly understood and practiced, it is not a grudging and distasteful plight but a gratifying and delightful privilege. Since this doctrine is part of God's infallible Word, there cannot be perfect harmony in marriage apart from its application. . . .
>
> How is this leadership implemented in the Christian home? I believe it is similar to the leadership exercised in any smoothly operating organization. No successful corporation can function properly with two heads. If there is a president and a vice-president, it is generally agreed that the president is the leader. The vice-president may actually be more brilliant than his boss, but the president still carries the greater authority. The arrangements will work best if there is a

mutual confidence and trust between them, if they look to each other as equals, if each shares and contributes from his own abilities, resources, and experiences, and if they mold policies and make decisions by mutual consent, with both men abiding by those decisions after they are made. Behind it all, however, there is a realization that only one of them is actually the leader. In the last analysis, it is he who is responsible for all that is done.

This is exactly how a Christian marriage should work. It could be described as a democracy with male leadership. Each mate should be concerned for the other and for the best interests of the marriage. This should be a mutual sharing in the making of decisions and the resolving of problems. Because each partner displays a genuine love for the other, irresolvable problems should be rare, but in those rare cases God says that the husband lovingly leads and the wife lovingly follows.

This is God's blueprint for the Christian home and is a long way from the perverted view that once considered women to be less than human. It is also a far cry from the equally dangerous modern philosophy which frees women from the responsibilities of the home, the kitchen, and the kids, and liberates them from their husband's authority.

A woman finds real equality and freedom when she assumes her God-given role as a helpmate, relying on the man God has given her and graciously submitting to him. He in turn tenderly loves her, cherishes her, protects her and provides for her. God planned the role of the man and the woman to dramatize the relationship between Christ and the Church. He asks us to glorify Him by accepting our roles willingly and fulfilling them faithfully.*

---

*From pages 55, 58, 59 of *Marriage Is For Love*, by Richard L. Strauss, © 1973 by Tyndale House Publishers, Wheaton, Illinois. Used by permission.

In Dennis Guernsey's book *Thoroughly Married,* a different approach to submission is explained. In Mr. Guernsey's mind,

> Submission in Christian marriage is not only to be voluntary, it is also to be a decision between equals. . . . In addition to voluntariness and equality is an even more important facet of the meaning of submission. It is that submission in Christian marriage is to be mutual.
>
> I have suggested that submission means to be responsive to the leadership of another. If submission is to be mutual, it would mean that there are areas in our family life where I am the leader and there are areas where my wife is the leader. There are times when we defer to one another.*

After studying the issue of submission as recorded in the Scriptures, I suggest that you and your spouse decide which interpretation is a workable solution for your marital relationship. This interpretation should be consistent with your interpretation of the Scriptures.

Whichever interpretation you select, it seems evident that in cases where conflicting views arise about a decision to be made within the marriage, the husband should make that decision, since God charges him with that responsibility.

6. God intends for us to maintain our relationship and not to dissolve it. God discourages divorce, as seen in Matthew 19:9, unless one party is guilty of fornication.

Since God is all-knowing, we must conclude that He is aware of the difficulties involved in maintaining an effective marriage. Yet because of His stand against divorce, we

---

*From *Thoroughly Married,* by Dennis Guernsey, © 1975. Used by permission of Word Books, Publisher, Waco, Texas.

must conclude that God expects us to work out our problems with His help.

7. God intends for us to accept ourselves. Psalms 139:13-16 states, "You made all the delicate, inner parts of my body, and knit them together in my mother's womb. Thank you for making me so wonderfully complex! It is amazing to think about. Your workmanship is marvelous—and how well I know it. You were there while I was being formed in utter seclusion! You saw me before I was born and scheduled every day of my life before I began to breathe. Every day was recorded in your Book!"

Much has been written about the inability of people to have a quality relationship with others until they are able to accept themselves. Yet how can we fail to accept ourselves when God Himself has taken such a personal interest in us?

8. Recognize that feelings, even anger, are legitimate.
Many Scriptures indicate that anger in itself is not wrong, but only our inability to handle it constructively.

9. Be honest and truthful in love. Ephesians 4:25 states, "Stop lying to each other; tell the truth, for we are parts of each other, and when we lie to each other we are hurting ourselves." Ephesians 4:29 states, "Don't use bad language. Say only what is good and helpful to those you are talking to, and what will give them a blessing." The first verse encourages truthfulness, and the second verse seems to be saying that we should use discretion in talking to other people, including our mates, and if what we're going to say does not improve the relationship, we should evaluate whether it should be said at all.

10. Recognize your responsibility and that of your mate as outlined by Christ.

A. *Husbands' Responsibilities*
   1. Ephesians 5:25 says, "And you husbands, show the same kind of love to your wives as Christ showed to the church when he died for her." Men are instructed to have a sacrificial type of love.
   2. Ephesians 5:26 says that men are to live as examples for their wives.
   3. First Timothy 5:8 states, "But anyone who won't care for his own relatives when they need help, especially those living in his own family, has no right to say he is a Christian. Such a person is worse than the heathen." A man is to cherish his family, provide for their needs, and stay actively involved in their life. Unfortunately, many men place service to the church above cherishing and being actively involved in their family's life. Some men look down with disdain on a fellowman who is having an affair out of marriage, yet they spend an enormous amount of time having affairs with some type of civic activity which takes them away from home and family obligations.
   4. A man must love his wife. Ephesians 5:25 states, "And you husbands, show the same kind of love to your wives as Christ showed to the church when he died for her" (TLB). Ephesians 5:28 says, "That is how husbands should treat their wives, loving them as part of themselves. For since a man and his wife are now one, a man is really doing himself a favor and loving himself when he loves his wife." Ephesians 5:33 says, "So again I say, a man must love his wife as a part of himself."
   5. A man should meet his wife's sexual needs. First Corinthians 7:4 states, "The wife does not have authority over her own body, but the husband does;

and likewise also the husband does not have authority over his own body, but the wife does" (NASB). Some interpret this verse to mean that one should look after his or her partner's interests, seeing to it that the partner's needs are met first.

B. Wives' Responsibilities
1. They are to be responsive to their husband's leadership. They are to respect their husbands. Ephesians 5:33 says, "And the wife must see to it that she deeply respects her husband —obeying, praising and honoring him." "Respect" rules out manipulative behavior of her husband, as encouraged in *The Total Woman*, authored by Marabel Morgan. You cannot respect a person whom you manipulate.
2. Wives are to love their husbands. Titus 2:4 states, "These older women must train the younger women to live quietly, to love their husbands and their children."

C. Mutual Responsibilities
1. Both men and women should strive to maintain their outward physical attractiveness. The Apostle Paul stated that women should "adorn themselves modestly and sensibly in seemly apparel, not with braided hair or gold or pearls or costly attire, but by good deeds, as befits those who profess religion." Where some think Paul is discouraging close attention to one's appearance, his use of the word "adorn" disclaims this, since "adorn" means to prepare and arrange oneself attractively, as a bride prepares herself for a groom. Both men and women should strive to maintain attractive appearances.

2. Both men and women also have the responsibility to maintain inward beauty. First Peter 3:4 states, "Be beautiful inside, in your hearts, with the lasting charm of a gentle and quiet spirit which is so precious to God."

11. Accept God's gift of unconditional love. First John 4:8 states, "But if a person isn't loving and kind, it shows that he doesn't know God—for God is love." In Richard Strauss's book entitled *Marriage Is For Love*, he states, "No human being in the world can originate true *agape*. *Agape* is given by God alone. In fact, God himself is *agape*. The Bible is filled with descriptions of God giving, sacrificing, and providing for sinners like ourselves. When we receive Jesus Christ as our Savior, God pours his *agape* into our inner being. We feel this warm love everywhere within us because God has given us the Holy Spirit to fill our hearts with his love. God's love is then displayed in our daily experience."* Romans 5:5 states, "Then, when that happens, we are able to hold our heads high no matter what happens and know that all is well, for we know how dearly God loves us, and we feel this warm love everywhere within us because God has given us the Holy Spirit to fill our hearts with his love" (TLB).

Accepting God's *agape* love adds a new dimension to our marriage.

The Great Physician has provided this prescriptive plan designed to develop marital fullness.

Many of us now need to evaluate our marriage relationship in light of God's prescription.

We must constantly be aware that God expects nothing

---

*From page 42 of *Marriage Is For Love*, by Richard Strauss, © 1973 by Tyndale House Publishers, Wheaton, Illinois. Used by permission.

less than a maximum human effort from each of us to contribute to the quality of our marital relationship.

Jesus said, "I have come that ye might have life, and that ye might have it more abundantly." Abundant means full, ample, profuse, rich, and bountiful. Can Jesus promise abundant life without our marriage relationship being included within that abundance? I think not. When Jesus says abundant, He must include His ordained institution of marriage.

God's prescription plus our committed efforts equals marital fullness.

How to Be a People Helper
by Dr. Gary Collins

Everyone you know has problems, and it's likely you can help them more than you realize.

Think about it! More "hurting" people are helped by friends, relatives, parents and business associates than by professional counselors. Even the counseling profession is facing this fact.

It is the objective of this book to help you be a better People Helper than you already are!
- Understand the principles of Christian discipleship—the basis of being a People Helper
- Become more sensitive to others' feelings
- Learn how to deal with "people problem" crises

Paper $3.98 DCOL05

PAK
DCOL05

BOOK
DCOL04

WORKBOOK
HCOL02

NEW!
What Wives Wish Their Husbands Knew About Women by Dr. James Dobson

Dr. Dobson's newest material is his best yet!

This series of tapes, I feel, is *the* most important work of my professional life. The recordings were motivated by the agitation and depression experienced by many women today, resulting from changing concepts of femininity and the breakdown in relationships between husbands and wives. Included in this album are the messages women most want their husbands to hear...and some important suggestions directly to wives, as well. If the listener can obtain only one of my albums, this should be it.

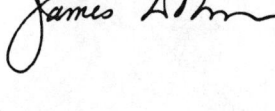

Biblical Lovemaking

by Tim Timmons
with Doug and Karen Wilson

God made man and woman for each other, to enjoy physically as well as psychologically, according to His principles given in the Bible. From his *Maximum Marriage* series, Tim expands this important theme on four cassettes, in cooperation with Doug and Karen Wilson. These intimate, frank, and problem-solving cassette messages will be more than helpful for "veterans" as well as newlyweds.

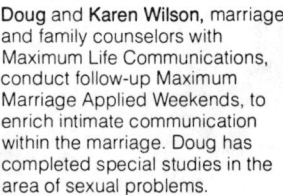

Tape Titles:
Physical Intimacy—*Tim Timmons*
Sexual Myths and the Foundation of Love—*Tim Timmons*
Basic Sexual Anatomy—*Doug and Karen Wilson (Side 1)*
Sexual Techniques—*Doug and Karen Wilson (Side 2)*
Basic Sexual Adjustments—*Doug and Karen Wilson*
4 Tapes $19.98 4TIM01

Doug and **Karen Wilson**, marriage and family counselors with Maximum Life Communications, conduct follow-up Maximum Marriage Applied Weekends, to enrich intimate communication within the marriage. Doug has completed special studies in the area of sexual problems.

Game Plan for Marriage
by Tim Timmons

Love means you never have to keep score! Tim Timmons contrasts the "competition and comparison" marriage with God's game plan for harmony, love and cooperation: "1 + 1 = 1." Solid, practical concepts packed into an easy-reading Slim Gem!
48-page Pocket paperback $.98 ATIM01
See page 37 for other Slim Gem titles.

Tim Timmons is the Director of Maximum Life Communications. He holds a Bachelor of Arts in communications from Cedarville College in Ohio and a Master of Theology in Greek from Dallas Theological Seminary.

Pursuing his gift of communication, Tim has spoken extensively in all parts of the country. He is presently conducting city-wide "Maximum Marriage" seminars throughout the world.

Tim has served as a part-time instructor in practical theology at Dallas Theological Seminary. He is the author of four books: *Chains of the Spirit: A Manual for Liberation, One Plus One, Maximum Marriage,* and *The Ultimate Lifestyle.*

151 Ways to a Better Life

There's a whole new world of reading and listening pleasure available to you, from Vision House Publishers and One Way Library. Discover all "151 Ways to a Better Life" in our convenient new catalog of books and cassettes. Send for your own complimentary copy today.

You'll find a large selection of fine Vision House products when you visit your local bookstore—or order directly from Vision House. Order forms are provided in our catalog.

VISION HOUSE PUBLISHERS
1507 East McFadden
Santa Ana, California 92705